Changing Hats

From Social Work Practice
to Administration

Changing Hats

From Social Work Practice
to Administration

Felice Davidson Perlmutter

NASW Press
National Association of Social Workers
Richard L. Edwards, President
Mark G. Battle, Executive Director

Library of Congress Cataloging-in-Publication Data

Perlmutter, Felice Davidson, 1931–
    Changing hats: From social work practice to administration /
Felice Davidson Perlmutter.
        p.   cm.
    Includes bibliographical references and index.
    ISBN 0-87101-184-0
    1. Social work administration—United States.   I. Title.
HV95.P47   1990
361.3′068—dc20   90-6436
                                                                        CIP

Printed in the U.S.A.

Cover and interior design by Ronna Hammer, Takoma Park, Md.

To Simon Slavin—
  Colleague, Mentor, and Friend
      and
To the Memory of Samuel Davidson—
  Father, Mentor, and Friend

Contents

Preface and Acknowledgments

Administration in social work is just coming into its own. Most managers have moved up the social agency ladder from direct practice and are unprepared for the dramatic personal, conceptual, and technical shifts that administration requires. Furthermore, for social workers in direct practice who have aspirations toward administration and for the majority of students in schools of social work who are specializing in direct practice, there is little available in the literature or in courses either to help them understand what administration is about or to help them decide whether administration is the professional route they should travel.

This book has two target populations. First, it is intended to be a resource for a broad audience of social workers who are seeking information about social work administration and to help them determine whether they wish to shift their career goals. Second, it is designed to serve as a textbook for students in direct practice social work programs, who should understand administration not only in terms of its relationship to enhancing service delivery but also as an important social work method.

The content in this volume is selective because it stems from and reflects my particular work and interests in the field as both a teacher and a researcher. It is based largely on my lectures, consultations, and publications. The individual chapters highlight theoretical and conceptual content and address some of the technical areas of administration. The case material is designed to provide a direct and accessible linkage to real-life situations.

This volume is organized as follows. Part I focuses on the theoretical aspects of social administration. The chapters in Part I examine the personal, systems, and organizational dimensions inherent in administrative social work practice. The discussion is relevant not only for aspiring administrators but also for those practicing administrators who have moved up the professional ladder from direct service positions and have had no formal preparation for or training in administration.

Part II presents a series of issues that reflect contemporary realities of the field. The discussion is applications-oriented and makes use of case material. The reader should feel free to use his or her own experience and organizational setting as case material on which to test the theory; both approaches to case material are meaningful for an individual's personal learning experience.

Part III shifts the discussion to a broader level. It highlights the importance of social work ethics for the effective practice of social work administration. It also introduces a future perspective as an essential administrative concern.

Changing Hats will meet its objective if it helps its readers clarify their career directions. For those who choose to embark on a career in administration, there is a vast literature to be explored, whether it be in formal educational settings or through independent study. This further exploration is essential for providing a broader and deeper understanding of social administration, in particular, and administration and management, in general.

There are, indeed, so many sources of encouragement and support in the process of completing a professional volume. First and foremost, I acknowledge the many students in my administration seminars in the master of social work program and in the Post-Masters Certificate Program at Temple University. We all struggled and learned through the process.

I also acknowledge my social work colleagues in both academe and social service agencies who are struggling to validate the practice of social work administration as an urgent priority for the social work profession.

Professor Bruno Scrosati generously made available clerical and computer facilities at the University of Rome during the summer of 1988. Patrizia Morghen, the office administrator, facilitated my work. Marianne Kilbride and Lillian Gibson helped with the final preparation of the manuscript at Temple University.

My children Shira, Saul, and Tova all provided critical assistance in different aspects of the manuscript's preparation. Their wise counsel is deeply appreciated.

And, finally, I thank my husband, Dan, who, as always and everywhere, is a constant source of support and encouragement.

F. D. P.

Part I Theoretical Perspectives

1

Introducing the Discussion

Changing Hats was deliberately chosen as the title for this book because it projects an image of choice. Implicit in this choice are the questions that social work practitioners must have clarified before they don an administrator's hat. Consequently, this first chapter is devoted to answering the immediate, and perhaps most obvious, questions.

WHAT IS UNIQUE ABOUT SOCIAL WORK ADMINISTRATION?

Social work practitioners have been drawn to the field because they are interested in working with people who are seeking to improve their lives. The client may be a widower with three children, who seeks personal service on a one-to-one basis. The client can be a group such as parents of gay children who are seeking support and help in accepting this reality. Or the client can be a larger group, such as southwest Germantown in Philadelphia, a neighborhood that has a large proportion of community-based housing for individuals in the mental health system and that is seeking to ensure neighborhood stability. The unifying thread that runs across all these examples is the direct contact between the social worker and the client–consumer.

Among the many ways by which social workers enter the field, there are three primary routes: Some have clearly selected social work for their professional career and have completed their master of social work degree; others have chosen social work as their undergraduate major and have earned a bachelor of social work degree; and yet others have entered the field by chance because of the availability of a job, although their undergraduate degree is either in a related discipline (for example, psychology or sociology) or even in an unrelated discipline (for example, literature or history).

Although most practitioners enjoy their direct service roles and seek to improve their repertoire of skills through continuing education in areas such as family therapy, supervision, or community organization, a small fraction of practitioners is attracted to administration. Yet, many practitioners in this small cohort feel both uninformed and insecure about this tentative preference.

Questions that illustrate these doubts are often raised by social work practitioners. "What do administrators do? Do I have the personality or style to be an administrator? Can I shift from direct practice to administration? Can I be an administrator if I am not experienced in financial matters?"

This book is designed to help practitioners and aspiring social work administrators who have these questions to explore the ins and outs of social work administration. It focuses on critical dimensions of administrative practice and seeks to broaden the reader's understanding of this specialization. It should help the reader come to an informed decision concerning the question: Should I become a social work administrator?

Before I go into this discussion further, it is important to present a working definition of social work administration. For the purposes of this volume, *social work administration* is leadership activity in social service agencies, both public and private, that makes possible the provision of services to client populations by translating social policy into social programs. The agencies can be either direct service or administrative-planning settings. It should be noted that the following terms are used interchangeably: voluntary agency, nonprofit agency, and private agency (in contrast to a public agency).

The focus here is primarily on central administration, first, because this is the arena in which policy is made and politics are played, and second, because theoretical underpinnings and the necessary skills are dramatically different from those in direct practice and will introduce the readers to new areas with which they are unfamiliar. Because most professionals enter administration through middle management, however, a chapter that focuses on the unique aspects of the middle manager's role is also included.

WHAT ARE THE BIASES?

A discussion of social work administration is enriched by an understanding of the underlying assumptions, biases, and preferences. These starting points are important for determining the approach to the material, and their clear recognition should help the reader read and digest the content critically.

The first assumption that underpins the discussion in this volume is that the route to social work administration is best traveled from the starting point of direct practice or experience in social service. An understanding of consumer needs, concerns, and problems provides a client orientation that Slavin (1980) suggests is indispensable for the practice of social work administration. This is counter to the view that training in business administration through a master of business administration (MBA) degree can most efficiently and effectively provide managerial leadership for all organizations.

Stanley Marcus, of the Nieman-Marcus department stores, agrees with Slavin, albeit from an altogether different point of reference. During the 1970s the stores hired people with MBAs from prestigious schools, because this was considered the best way to ensure effective management. Marcus then found that business training in the abstract was not the best option. Even in business enterprises, in this case, the Nieman-Marcus stores, knowledge of and experience in the particular venture are essential; any further education in administration must occur over and above this fundamental background.

Thus, the candidate most suitable for moving up into the executive suite is the practitioner who has had several years of hands-on experience in the field. Although this experience is necessary, it is insufficient. Specialized education in administration must provide the appropriate theoretical, analytical, and technical skills necessary for performing the broad array of administrative roles.

The second assumption that underpins this discussion is that the role of the social work administrator is a proactive one, a role that provides leadership in the broadest sense. Not only is it necessary to keep the shop running smoothly and efficiently today to meet current needs, but it is also necessary to have a vision of and anticipate what is possible and necessary for tomorrow.

In his classic volume *Leadership in Administration*, Selznick (1957) articulates this viewpoint beautifully:

> If one of the great functions of administration is the exertion of cohesive force in the direction of institutional security, another great function is the creation of conditions that will make possible in the future what is excluded in the present. This requires a strategy of change that looks to the attainment of new capabilities more nearly fulfilling the truly felt needs and aspirations of the institution. (pp. 153–154)

It should be noted that Selznick's view of proactive leadership is not unique to social work administration, but it is implicit in all areas of administrative practice, whether it be in the public or private sector.

Theoretical Perspectives

The third assumption, which is directly related to the principle of proactive leadership, is that social work administrators must serve as advocates for the constituency they serve. This entails an ongoing commitment not only to informing the broader society about the clientele they serve but also to demanding more responses and resources on their behalf. Although advocacy is recognized, in general, as an essential element by the social work profession, it is all too often neglected when social work administrators are caught up in responding to countless immediate pressures.

The Ad Hoc Committee on Advocacy, appointed by the National Association of Social Workers (NASW) in 1968, recognized this special obligation of the administrator and addressed the issue directly. The administrator "is bound to act as an advocate on behalf of clients under his jurisdiction. A collateral obligation would be the responsibility of the supervisor or administrator to create the climate in which direct-service workers can discharge their advocacy obligations" (Ad Hoc Committee on Advocacy, 1969, p. 18).

This does not mean to imply that administrative advocacy is simple to achieve or is without risks. What is important to acknowledge is that all organizations are stimulated to change when risk-taking and advocacy permeate their agendas. Nonetheless, administrative advocacy is, indeed, a distinguishing characteristic of social work administration.

The fourth assumption, which is related to advocacy, is that the empowerment of staff and client-consumers is an administrative responsibility. Given the enormous pressures faced by administrators, it is often simpler to yield to the temptation to take charge, to make decisions, to go it alone. This runs counter to the well-established social work value of client self-determination, which is succinctly stated in the NASW (1979) *Code of Ethics:* "The social worker should make every effort to foster maximum self-determination on the part of clients" (p. 1).

The professional concern with and acceptance of the value of self-determination must be duly heeded by the administrator who is working with highly trained professionals. The challenge is one of translating beliefs into practice. The concept of empowerment flows directly from this professional requisite, and it is the responsibility of the social work administrator to broaden this focus on the client to include all levels of staff as well. The notion of administrative responsibility for staff and client empowerment is also a unique and distinguishing characteristic of social work administration.

These four assumptions should be kept in mind while reading the chapters that follow. The administrator who is experienced, proactive, advocating, and empowering is the ideal type for dealing with the varied issues and dilemmas encountered in the practice of social work administration and is the actor who will be discussed in this volume. In fact, the unique identity of social work administration may flow from these assumptions and may well serve to answer the following question: How is social work administration different from management in general?

WHAT IS THE THRUST OF THIS BOOK?

The ability to understand theory and to be able to apply it provides the social work administrator with great flexibility. This book will present selected theoretical concepts that are important for administration and will illustrate them with case material from an array of social work settings. Whereas some of the material is generic and is applicable across all settings, other portions are specific to a particular situation and were selected so that they highlight that particular concept.

This volume focuses on both theory and practice, because theory informs practice. Not only does it open the door to a consideration of new vistas, but it also creates the opportunity for creative choice and provides the social work administrator with a wider range of options.

A BRIEF NOTE ABOUT THEORY

Professions are governed by general principles, or theories, that serve as a guide for practitioners in the plying of their craft. Just as artists must first be trained in the techniques of their discipline before they develop their individual styles and creativities, so, too, must social work administrators be schooled in the theories that interpret and explain the events in their domain before they can develop innovative and effective solutions. The comparison of social work administration with music and art is useful in that creativity and individual style in all these cases reflect excellence in performance.

Social workers are aware of and informed about the various theories that create a framework for their work. Furthermore, they are aware of the fact that different practitioners in the same field prefer and use different theoretical models as the basis for their practices. For example, therapists may be Freudian, Ericksonian, or behaviorist, and recently many therapists have dramatically shifted their theoretical approaches to reflect a family therapy model. Even within the emerging field of family therapy, there are different theories that inform practice and that reflect the views of different theoreticians such as Minuchin (1974), Bowen (1978), or the Milano school (Selvini-Palazzoli, Boscolo, Cecchin, & Prata, 1978).

In group work and in community organization, there is also an array of theoretical models that serve as a guide for the practitioner. Community organization based on an Alinsky (1946) radical activist model differs from community organization based on the Rothman (1974) planning model or the Ross (1967) community integration model.

The benefits of a theoretical framework that can serve as a guide for the social work administrator can be highlighted. Administration is a complex process that requires constant decision making on a broad array of problems; it is tempting, and not unusual, to make these decisions on an ad hoc basis to meet immediate needs and thereby to reduce pressure. A theoretical model helps the administrator to redefine the problem and to formulate a solution that is appropriate for the organization.

In all cases, regardless of the field, the administrator should not work only from an idiosyncratic, or "gut," sense; the work must also reflect an approach that has been tested in the broader community of ideas. A theory provides guidelines for professional analysis and action.

In any discussion of theory, however, it is important to point out that although theory seeks to explain behavior, it is not the same as a scientifically proven law. With this proviso, it is useful to note that the practitioner is operating in a flexible context and has freedom to choose that which seems appropriate and useful. For example, in the field of medicine, in seeking to prevent osteoporosis, some gynecologists recommend that their patients take vitamin C, others recommend vitamin C with estrogen, and some are unsure whether either course should be taken. Because the evidence is inconclusive, the choice is an individual one and ends up depending on the patient, the doctor, or both. This contrasts with the use of the polio vaccine for the prevention of polio, for which the scientific evidence is definitive.

An example in social work administration is the use of the theory of self-management, or participatory democracy, as the basis of decision making in the social service agency. Although this theory may be compatible with social work values, its utilization must be understood in relation to the specific organizational setting (Pusic, 1974).

Sherman (1966), former head of New York City's transportation system, argues that although it is important to be informed about

8

theory, the bottom line for effective administration is to tailor the solution to the particular problem and the particular setting. The title of his book, *It All Depends*, clearly reflects his viewpoint. A slavish adherence to theory is a foolish consistency, but the external perspective provided by theory can create the possibility of a more liberated and flexible leadership.

Theory serves another crucial function. It is very easy for beleaguered executives to personalize the problems they are dealing with and to experience personal discomfort. A theoretical awareness helps the administrator to generalize the analysis, to depersonalize the process, and to view the problem as an expected and universal occurrence.

CONCLUSION

It is exciting to contemplate a career in social work administration. For some social workers, the possibility of providing better services to clients by helping to make the agency work more effectively and efficiently is challenging. The prospect of entering into a new, yet not entirely different, arena while learning new theory and skills is equally challenging.

Of course, there are "different strokes for different folks." The trick is to discover which route maximizes personal preference and satisfaction, attributes that are essential to be effective professionally.

This volume will expose the reader to new ideas, methodologies, technologies, and dilemmas. It should soon be clear to the reader whether this material is relevant. If it is, the reader stands ready to contemplate new career directions in the field of social work.

2

The Context of Social
Work Administration

As a social work method, social work administration operates within the external societal and the internal professional contexts. The administrator is the bridge between the two, and accordingly he or she must be sensitive and responsive to both.

THE SOCIETAL CONTEXT

U.S. society is experiencing an exponential rate of social change that affects not only the management of social service but also management in all sectors of society (Skinner & Sasser, 1977). The focus of this chapter is on some of the contextual realities that are of primary concern to the social work administrator.

The Turbulent Environment

In an early paper that is a classic in the organizational literature, Emery and Trist (1969) identify the environment of an organization as being critical to an understanding of its behavior, because not only the organization but also the environment in which it is embedded are in constant flux. Although Emery and Trist focus on the economic sector, their typology of environments is equally applicable to the social welfare sector.

The simplest environments are placid and relatively unchanging. There are two types of placid conditions: type 1, in which the environment is scattered and random, requiring only an ad hoc, situational response appropriate for small, simple, and flexible organizational units, and type 2, in which there is a clustering of environmental needs and in which organizations must respond in a more distinctive and directed manner. "Organizations under these conditions . . . tend to grow in size and also to become hierarchical, with a tendency toward centralized control and co-ordination" (Emery & Trist, 1969, p. 247).

The other two environments are dynamic and are distinguished primarily by their complexity. In type 3 environments, a number of competitive organizations arise, and dealing with competition becomes a primary organizational focus. In type 4 environments, the environment is identified as one of turbulence accompanied by areas of relative uncertainty. There is a "deepening interdependence between the economic and other facets of the society. . . . Economic organizations are increasingly enmeshed in legislation and public regulation" (Emery & Trist, 1969, p. 249). There is an "increasing reliance on research and development to achieve the capacity to meet competitive challenge" (p. 249).

U.S. society is currently experiencing a type 4 turbulent environment, which was certainly not always the case in the development of social welfare programs in the twentieth century (Leiby, 1987). That the social work administrator is dramatically affected by this turbulence is illustrated in a poignant letter written to the author by a social work administrator:

> As you may know, I came into administration like most executives of my vintage—through the skill of being a pretty good practitioner and then a good supervisor. . . . Fortunately I did come into the job as executive . . . when there was still the usual rhythm of going on year to year, and changes, if they occurred, took about 2 to 4 years and you had a lot of time to get used to them. I don't believe that there is any place in the country that such a rhythm is possible, today, at least, if one is going to survive.

It must be noted that this letter was written in the early 1970s, when pressures on social service agency administrators were just beginning to escalate. This was a time when the federal government entered the social service field with its demands for proposals to obtain public funds and with the new expectations of accountability (Newman & Turem, 1974). Yet, in comparison with today's pressures, that decade seems placid.

The Changing Value System

A major source of the background turbulence in U.S. society is the dramatic shifts in the value system that supports social service. The fact that every 4 to 8 years a new president and that every 2 years a new U.S. Congress can completely reverse the intent of the predecessors creates great pressures and tensions in the social service system. One only needs to look at the decimation of the poverty program, community legal services, community mental health, and housing and urban development, to cite a few, to recognize that the cost of political change is great.

Not only is the rate of change in the public mandate great, but of even greater significance is the change in the public mood vis-à-vis social policies and programs. In a provocative paper, Stern (1984) argues that these shifts are predictable and that the American people are basically conservative and unwilling to commit themselves to a welfare state ideology. He suggests that the programs developed in the 50-year period between the New Deal of Franklin D. Roosevelt and the Great Society of Lyndon B. Johnson responded to emergency circumstances and reflect the efforts of an unusual coalition of bureaucrats and special interest groups.

> Thus, political capitalism's legitimacy is not based, as is social democracy's, on a critique of capitalism. Rather, it attempts to make minor corrections in a social system that is assumed "naturally" to work well.
>
> Even this rather restricted view of the interventionist state is not particularly popular with voters in American popular culture. In bad times, government action could gain public and congressional support because "something had to be done," but in better times, the appeals of self-reliance, the work ethic, and negative stereotypes of the poor made federal social-welfare actions less palatable. (p. 5)

Although the conflict in values and the political shifts experienced on a regular basis affect all of the helping professions, social welfare programs are most vulnerable because they are the direct products of the social philosophy and fiscal policies of federal, state, and county governments. Stern (1984) suggests that the United States is in for a long siege by the conservative environment that was made conspicuous in the Reagan era. Although a new set of skills may be necessary to help administrators "minimize the adverse effects on client populations . . . , if the only actions of social welfare administrators are directed at these narrow goals, we will have won some battles and lost the war. Administrators must simultaneously focus on broad issues of social justice" (p. 19). This supports the proactive, advocacy approach discussed in Chapter 1.

A case example illustrates the effect of ideology on administrative choices and describes a reactive, rather than a proactive, administrator. A nationally renowned and respected social work administrator who was employed in a very prestigious private social service agency unwittingly described the details of the destruction of the integrity of the agency, its mandate, and its mission. In the quest for efficiency, the agency's effectiveness was lost when the administrator convinced the board of directors to shift agency priorities from serving Medicaid-eligible patients to serving middle-class, insured populations who could generate third-party payments. When asked what would happen to the poor who needed the agency's service, the response was: "I can't carry them on my back." Clearly, this was not an easy matter, and the agency was under financial pressure, but an effective leader with the attributes discussed earlier would indeed have sought a different solution.

The value framework that underpins administrative decision making is a critical one, comparable with the value framework that informs the mission of the agency. In this case, both were misplaced when the administrator did not address the adverse effects on the agency's original clientele.

The Changing Technology

The rapidly changing technology witnessed in the past decade is another factor that should be considered. The nature of administration in all sectors has been changed dramatically with the advent of computers. Computers have taken over many people's functions and have even been deified in U.S. society. Although the benefits are great, Gruber, Caputo, and Meenaghan (1984) and Wilson (1980) have called attention to the risks.

Gruber and colleagues provide a reminder that in an attempt to become management science oriented, and even "tough-minded," social work administrators in the 1970s and 1980s rushed to adopt wholesale the technical solutions and expertise provided by management consultants. The advice was not always appropriate or relevant, and in many instances it was even wasteful. Frequently, new consultants had to be hired, initial systems had to be discarded, and new systems had to be put on-line, all at great cost. Social workers were worried, however, that they might be seen as inefficient and inadequately accountable for their agencies' performance; as a result, many administrators were all too ready to accept uncritically the experts' advice.

Gruber and colleagues have developed a model by which the design of management information systems (MIS) is "characterized by open and egalitarian participation. . . . A strong commitment to definable ends and purposes will enable the MIS to serve as an electronic-age facilitation device" (pp. 140–141) to enhance rather than to replace effective leadership.

Wilson (1980) has expanded the discussion to encompass all technical components that are currently available to the administrator. In an important paper, he links the new technology with social work administrators' value systems and responsibilities for advocacy. The capacity to blend these diverse elements is the challenge to social work administrators.

Equal Opportunity Practices

Another factor for consideration arises from the observation that human resources in social service are also undergoing many changes related to the external environment. The topic of human resources is a broad one and can include, among other topics, personnel administration, employee motivation, and remuneration and benefits. The discussion here focuses on the increasing presence and new consciousness concerning women and minorities in management. These are addressed separately to highlight the particular concerns.

Social work has traditionally been identified as a female-dominant profession. Yet, the data show that despite the feminist movement, the proportion of females in social work administration has actually declined over the years. Furthermore, female administrators earn significantly lower salaries than do their male counterparts (Alexander & Kerson, 1980).

Although much attention has been given to the attitudes and behaviors of females who wish to succeed in administration, emphasis has been placed on career development through courses focused on assertiveness training and conquering the fear of success. This approach has only served to perpetuate a sterotype of the female administrator as imitating the aggressive male executive (for example, Henning & Jardim, 1977). By contrast, Kanter (1977) has focused on a structural model that addresses the organizational characteristics that impede or that are conducive to opportunities in management.

Alexander and Kerson (1980) have developed the structural argument further and address the consequences for social work agencies that want to remedy this situation. They suggest various strategies, including job redesign, job rotation, flexible working hours, and new ladders for access to managerial positions (pp. 205–207). The major importance of day care at the work place is also highlighted. It is not enough to mouth a rhetoric concerning good intentions; the proof of the pudding is in the eating.

In a discussion of the minority administrator, Vargus (1980) identifies some of the obstacles and dilemmas faced by nonwhite social work administrators "in order to sensitize all administrators and boards to the roles, conflicts, and contributions of the minority administrator" (p. 217).

Beginning with the hiring process, the external context creates a pressure as affirmative action programs engender reactions among nonminority colleagues that are frequently not expressed openly. Is the minority administrator hired for his or her competence or primarily as a gesture to the minority community and funding agency? Once in the position, is the administrator overidentified with his or her own minority group? Does the minority administrator have to continuously be a superachiever to gain acceptance? Is the minority administrator expected to play a buffer or liaison role with the minority community over and above the normal expectations of the position? Do the minority group members expect the minority administrator to be a strong advocate on their behalf?

Vargus suggests an array of coping mechanisms for the minority administrator. First, the minority administrator must be ready to engage in ongoing interpretation of his or her role by actively "educating others to the differences for minorities and therefore for himself or herself in the system. . . . This opens the door for greater communication and for sharing insights, and can save the institution embarrassment"(p. 224). Second, Vargus stresses the importance of support groups comprising minority administrators in which they can discuss unique problems and brainstorm. This strategy is important for all administrators. Third, the minority administrator must become comfortable in the use of authority, which is again a problem for all clinicians who move into administration, but this is highlighted by Vargus in relation to "those situations where the administrator believes that racism is operating" (p. 226). Finally, Vargus discusses the importance of skills in negotiation and communication, which are essential for all administrators but are of particular importance for community- and organization-based, complex situations that may arise, especially in the area of race negotiations.

It is important to emphasize that all social work administrators must be aware of the special concerns of women and minorities, especially as they move up the organizational ladder, and must seek appropriate solutions that can pave the way for the more active development of a cadre of female and minority social work administrators.

Union Negotiations

The growth of unions is taking hold among many professional groups, including social workers, in both the public and the voluntary sectors (Aronson, 1985). The negotiation process inherent in collective bargaining is the direct responsibility of the social work administrator.

The administrator often experiences personal conflicts regarding this process for several reasons. First, it is not surprising that conflict occurs because, frequently, the social work administrator has been a supporter of the trade union movement either on an abstract, ideological level or on a direct, personal level as a staff member of a professional local. Being placed in the adversarial role of administrator can create great personal tensions as one crosses the picket line or even sits across the bargaining table as the representative of management. Second, social work administrators often view themselves as devoted to and involved with their staffs and are consequently unprepared for the feelings of rejection and betrayal they experience when their staff members decide to unionize.

In either case, it is essential that the administrator recognize and deal with these feelings. A wonderful example is provided by an administrator who has always been an active union supporter. Yet, during a long-term strike, he went to his office regularly, covered the telephones, and did what was necessary to keep the agency functioning at a minimal level. When asked by his young associate how he dealt with the conflict inherent in the situation, he responded that his role was that of administrator and that the different parties had their own roles to play. There was never any acrimony in his attitude as he met his staff members. This was in sharp contrast to another administrator who was angry, felt betrayed, and developed serious physical symptoms because he personalized the process.

The bottom line for the social work administrator is dealing fairly with the staff, being aware of the best pay and benefits packages in the geographic area, and playing an active role with the board of directors in interpreting an appropriate response. This is an unexplored area, and there is a need for more serious attention to the administrative responsibility in collective bargaining, both in research and practice (Alexander, 1987).

THE PROFESSIONAL CONTEXT

As a specialization within the social work profession, social work administration is still struggling to find its place. Although some writings on social work administration were published as early as the 1940s (Dunham, 1941; Trecker, 1948), and although the Council on Social Work Education sponsored an extensive study and published its findings on administration as a field of practice only a decade later (Spencer, 1959), social work administration is still struggling to become part of the professional mainstream of social work.

Gummer (1979), in a trenchant analysis of the plight of social work administrators in the public sector, identifies them as an "endangered species." This designation is apt not only for administrators in the public sector but also for social work administration in general. This leads to a focus on the problems created internally within a profession that is unprepared to face the fact that social work administrators operate on a different level and have different needs and priorities than those of their professional staff.

This problem is the subject of an article entitled "Beyond Parochialism in Social Welfare Administration" in which Carroll (1978) traces the development of social work administration. She suggests that the "road to recognition has been rocky, characterized more by reluctance than eagerness on the part of the profession" (p. 31). She notes that despite the historical fact that administrators of social agencies typically came up through the staff ranks and were trained in direct service methods, it was not until 1967 that the National Association of Social Workers issued a position paper accepting administration as an area of social work practice.

It is instructive to attempt to understand this reluctance to deal with it more effectively. The following issues are highlighted because they are indicative of the dilemmas, tensions, constraints, and conflicts in which administrative practice in social work is embedded. Although these issues are posed as questions, they are directly related to administrative performance and to the elements identified earlier as being critical to the external context. These issues illustrate the facts not only that professional preparation is needed that is different from that which prepares social workers for direct practice, but also that ongoing professional development is different.

Politics versus professionalism: Given the increased politicization of social service, can a social work administrator protect the integrity of his or her professional commitments and concerns?

Accountability: Although social work administrators have traditionally focused on accountability to their clients, new discussions of accountability introduce new debates in this area. Are public social service agencies accountable to the taxpayer (Bledsoe, Denny, Hobbs, & Long, 1972) as opposed to the client?

Efficiency versus effectiveness: Social work administrators are under continuous pressure to focus on efficiency because "economy and efficiency are salient issues" (Lynn, 1980, p. 19). How can the concern with meeting client needs be optimized within this reality context?

Bureaucratization versus debureaucratization: What organizational design is appropriate for the diverse programs in social service? What is the appropriate model for organizational decision making, given the importance of the organizational environment?

Technology: Given the continuous developments in administrative technologies, as discussed earlier, how does the social work administrator make the appropriate decisions in the use of the technologies and in the selection of consultants or technical experts?

The declining societal commitment to social work: Because social work may be an "endangered species," what is the responsibility of the social work administrator both inside and outside the organizational setting?

The professional use of self: What are the essential interpersonal skills needed not only to maximize the effectiveness of the administrator's role, but also to empower agency staff in their working environment?

These issues are indeed critical ones, and social work administrators must be prepared to deal with them. This requires a different knowledge base, a different set of skills, and different educational preparation.

WHAT ARE THE IMPLICATIONS OF THIS DISCUSSION?

Leadership in social work administration is critical for the success of social welfare programs in terms of both efficiency and effectiveness. The problems created for social work administration are complex and stem from external as well as internal forces.

In addition to the complexity described above, the administration of social programs in both the public and the private sectors is suddenly of interest to an array of new stakeholders. These stakeholders are primarily concerned with fiscal rather than client priorities. It is not surprising that, in the desperate effort to curtail costs, boards of directors of social service agencies have looked to business administrators to solve their agencies' fiscal problems. The problems remain complex, however, and resolution of these problems is not clear cut.

What is clear is that social work administration requires a broad array of competencies, in addition to ideological commitments and service delivery skills. The challenges are great for the social work profession to retain leadership in the field, and opportunities are numerous for creative and charismatic leadership. It is also clear, however, that administration is not for the faint of heart; rather, it is for those who are heartened by these provocative and demanding situations and who are ready to attain the competencies requisite to the task.

3

Making the Shift from Practice to Administration

Two questions frequently asked by social work practitioners—"Would I enjoy administration?" and "Would I be effective as a social work administrator?"—reflect genuine confusion that results from several factors. Knowledge about what the administrator actually does is often unclear. The technical aspects of administration are unfamiliar and often threatening. The practitioner is in conflict about abandoning the client caseload but is simultaneously driven by the hope that his or her leadership can make things work better in the agency. The conflict is unfortunately exacerbated by the occasional negative perceptions and administrators who are viewed in an adversarial role.

This chapter seeks to reduce confusion by addressing two topics of major importance. The first is the personal perspective that is essential in making the shift from practice to administration. The second is the systems perspective that is essential to performing the role of administrator.

THE PERSONAL PERSPECTIVE

In a personal account entitled "On Becoming an Agency Executive," Elbow (1975) effectively documents and illustrates the confusion that accompanies the process of "changing hats." After being promoted up the ranks to the position of executive director, she still believed that her most important work was with her client caseload; the administrative duties were necessary, but they had to be endured and dispensed with as quickly as possible. Consequently, she allocated 25 percent of her time to working with clients.

Furthermore, Elbow continued to have lunch and socialize with her colleagues, retaining them as her professional network, a network of long standing. At the same time, she felt that she was not in control of her work; was overwhelmed by the pressures; and was uncomfortable with the role, the power, and the authority inherent in it.

It took a full 18 months for her to gain the insights necessary to make the shift from direct service to administration, a shift that is all too often not made by practitioners who come up the organizational ladder. First, she recognized that as the agency administrator she would most effectively serve the clients as an advocate for all of them. She realized that by retaining a caseload, she was focusing on her particular clients and, as a result, was abdicating her role as administrative advocate for the total system.

Second, she recognized that her professional network would have to change: She needed to develop relationships with administrators outside of her own organization with whom she could share ideas, discuss problems, and brainstorm. Third, she accepted the consequences of these two shifts: She would not only have more time to focus on her administrative tasks, but she would also make the emotional separation that is necessary in coming to grips with the reality of administrative power and authority.

The trauma in making the shift from direct service to administration is not unique for social workers. It is common to all professionals trained to be direct service or clinically oriented. In fact, Levinson and Klerman (1967) suggest that this shift is as difficult and complicated as any developmental transition in the normal life cycle, such as adolescence, marriage, widowhood, or old age, and can be accompanied by depression or other internally disruptive responses. Consequently, it is important to understand the dynamics implicit in the shift so that the process of changing hats can be least disruptive.

A major source of the difficulty is the fact that completely different skills and orientations are appropriate for these diverse roles. For example, the direct service practitioner focuses on the particular, be it an individual, group, or community, as opposed to the administrator, who focuses on the general (that is, the system). The practitioner works directly with the client by using a hands-on approach, in contrast to the administrator, who delegates much of the work. The practitioner responds to the immediate situation, whereas the administrator must set priorities. The practitioner is often an enabler and is neutral in orientation, whereas the administrator must take a stand and provide leadership. The clinician is often passive and facilitating, in contrast to the administrator, who is active. The practitioner is oriented to the present, in contrast to the administrator, who is oriented to the future. Perhaps the most important and, according to

Theoretical Perspectives

Levinson and Klerman, most difficult difference is that the practitioner is unschooled and uncomfortable in the use of power and authority, whereas the most characteristic expectation of the administrator is the exercise of authority and the use of power.

Levinson and Klerman offer an interesting and powerful model in their presentation of a synthesis of the position of clinician–administrator. They suggest that the appropriate use of clinical perspectives and skills can enhance administrative performance. They present a series of "role tasks" that the new administrator should aim to master to assume the new role effectively. Although their discussion focused directly on the psychiatrist as administrator within the context of a psychiatric facility, the role tasks that are presented are appropriate for the social worker as administrator in a social agency setting.

Their first role task is that of "developing an integrated social-and-psychological conception of the organization and its societal context" (p. 56). Although the administrator can make use of his or her background in and understanding of personality theory and interpersonal relations, the administrator's attention must be directed to understanding the organization as a social system and the behavior of bureaucracy. They cite sociology, anthropology, and political science as bodies of knowledge relevant to the administrator's role. This first role task is broad and serves as the theoretical foundation for more specific tasks. A discussion of specific role tasks is provided later in this chapter.

Levinson and Klerman's second role task is dealing with other staff members from a position of authority. Because administrators have authority over many subordinates in the system, decisions must constantly be made not only about administrative matters (for example, budgets and resources) but also about personnel issues, promotions, dismissals, and salaries. The problem of authority is even more complicated in professional settings, in which there are two types of authority: one that flows from the bureaucratic arrangements in the organization and a second one that flows from the expertise of the professional. Because the essence of professionalism is the exercise of autonomous judgment, the use of administrative authority is not clear cut and varies according to the setting and the stage of the organization's development within that setting (Chapter 4 discusses organization development in greater detail).

A third role task is that of relating to members of other professions and disciplines. Although Levinson and Klerman focus on these relationships within the psychiatric setting, social workers are also continuously involved with various professionals, including, among others, teachers, physicians, psychiatrists, and community organizers. This entails a sensitivity not only to the different goals and techniques inherent in these diverse groups, but also to their different value frameworks.

Dealing with people, groups, and institutions outside one's organization, the fourth role task identified by Levinson and Klerman, requires a broad and flexible stance. The administrator must work with public agencies, local governments, foundations, community groups, the news media, and a host of other systems that have contact with the agency.

A fifth role task, providing for organizational growth and innovation, is a major focus throughout this volume. Friesen and Austin (1984) suggest that "a framework for proactive administration is represented by the acronym, VISION, which stands for Values, Intent, Skills, Innovation, Objectives, and Negotiation" (p. 184).

The final role task for the administrator is achieving a new identity. Once the developmental transition has taken place, a new identity is achieved. This transition was successfully made by Elbow (1975) as discussed above. Although it took her 18 months to achieve a new identity and to realize that she did not have to carry a caseload to effectively serve the agency's clients, once the recognition took place, it affected all aspects of her performance.

In 1972, 5 years after their earlier article, Levinson and Klerman wrote another piece entitled "The Clinician-Executive Revisited." Although they reaffirmed the importance of the earlier discussion, they added a new emphasis:

> An essential (though often neglected) requirement of top management is that it concern itself chiefly with the management of external boundaries. The concept of external boundary is a crucial one in organizational analysis. An organization exists within a large and complex environment. . . . If the organization is to survive and flourish, it must obtain numerous inputs (finances, clients, students, staff, prestige, moral as well as legal support, knowledge) from surrounding systems and it must in turn export valued outputs to those systems. Its relationship with each adjacent system may be regarded as an ongoing set of transactions across a boundary. It is chiefly the responsibility of top management to create appropriate boundary structures and to ensure the necessary flow of inputs and outputs. (p. 66)

Only recently has it been recognized that the administrator must be externally oriented and must expend most of his or her energy outside the organization, within the broader arena that has a direct impact on the social service agency. The need for social work administrators to provide a link to external systems was discussed in Chapter 2, which focused on the context of social work administration. The shift in professional style and behaviors necessitated by an externally oriented approach will be central to subsequent chapters.

Gummer (1984) points out that the consequence of these external requirements is that the administrator must become sophisticated in organizational politics, effectively negotiating the political realities that affect the social service agency. According to Gummer, there are two dimensions to organizational politics: "the first involves an approach to organizational decision-making and the second concerns the acquisition, maintenance, and use of power within an organization" (p. 24). Both dimensions are central to administrative leadership and require skill in negotiation, mediation, and communication.

Social workers are all aware of the many interests and diverse positions within the social service agencies in which they work, but they may not be aware of the fact that negotiating this diversity is a political process. Furthermore, because all social service agencies, whether in the public or the private sector, are directly affected by social policies, the social work administrator is automatically thrust into the world of politics. This applies to all levels—local, state and federal—of government.

Levinson and Klerman (1972) inject a note of humor into their discussion of power and politics. They point out that mental health professionals view power and politics much as the people in Victorian England viewed sex: "It is seen as vulgar, as a sign of a character defect, as something an upstanding professional would not be interested in or stoop to engage in" (p. 66). Precisely because it is essential to recognize that for administrators political behavior is a fact of life, the relationship between professionalism and politics is the subject of Chapter 7.

In the earlier discussion of the unique characteristics of social work administration, the advocacy role was highlighted. There is a direct linkage between advocacy and politics because the administrator bears the responsibility of educating the broader community about the agency's experience regarding client needs. At the same time, the administrator must be skillful in challenging the community to accept a stake in the agency's mandate.

All too often the administrator is not clear on the political strategies implicit in advocacy. This was documented in a demonstration project in a public assistance agency that had advocacy as a major goal (Kronick, Perlmutter, & Gummer, 1973). Advocacy was to permeate the total agency and not just be the responsibility of individually dedicated caseworkers. Yet, when welfare recipients were ready and eager to take jobs in a neighboring community and no public transportation was available for the night shift for which there were openings, the agency statistical records only recorded that there were "unmet needs."

Thus, the administrator was negligent not only in regard to the design of appropriate management information forms that could document this client reality, but also in regard to the lack of use of political skills to bring about better availability of appropriate means of transportation (for example, minivans or swing-shift buses). She should have been an active advocate, especially because the purpose was to help welfare clients become economically self-supporting. Her inability to carry out this step represents a missed opportunity, particularly because it supported the community ideology vis-à-vis welfare.

In summary, it is apparent that a different set of orientations, skills, and expectations exists for the social work administrator than for the direct service practitioner. Nevertheless, it is, in fact, possible to make the shift successfully, because effective social work administration is built on direct practice experience.

THE SYSTEMS PERSPECTIVE

The first role task of the administrator identified by Levinson and Kerman (1967) is that of "developing an integrated social-and-psychological conception of the organization and its societal context" (p. 56). This can be identified as a systems perspective.

An understanding of the context of the social service agency is the starting point for effective administration, as discussed in Chapter 2. That discussion focused on five factors in the external environment that affect the social agency directly: (1) the turbulent environment, (2) value shifts, (3) new technology, (4) equal opportunity practices, and (5) professional unions. This section focuses on the primary constituents that make up the agency as a system and that are directly related to the first role task identified above.

Slavin (1980) presents a clear and comprehensive formulation of the social agency as a social system. He suggests that "all service-giving organizations combine three essential elements: the provider of the service (practitioner), the user of the service (client, consumer), and the organization (the service agency) that brings these two together" (p. 7). Each of these three elements is embedded in a network that not only impinges on them but also affects the agency. For example, the practitioner does not just operate as a worker in the organization but is connected to and identified with the profession for which he or she has been educated; the client has linkages both to a network of family and friends and to other clients who are experiencing the same problem; the agency is part of a community that is located either in the public or the voluntary sector.

Slavin explores these three elements and their networks in detail and orders them into primary, secondary and tertiary constituencies, depending on the intensity of the relationship and the connectedness of the elements. The primary constituencies are internal ones that are usually viewed as an administrative priority. Although the secondary and tertiary constituencies are external, as part of the larger social system of the agency, they also require direct administrative attention. Figure 3-1 is a graphic presentation of Slavin's (1980) concept of the "organizational life space" (p. 11) of the social service agency.

The applicability of these concepts can be explored through a case study. But before the concepts are discussed, the specific agency under analysis should be described.

Figure 3-1. Organizational Life Space of Social Administration: The Constituencies of the Social Administrators

	PRACTITIONER (provider) ↔	ORGANIZATION (social agency) ↔	CLIENT (consumer)
	↓	↓	↓
PRIMARY (internal) constituencies	Staff system	Trustee system	Client system
	↓	↓	↓
SECONDARY (external) constituencies*	Professional associations, labor unions, alumni	Institutional network, federations, funding agencies, coordinating bodies	Parent associations, consumer groups, special interest groups
	↓	↓	↓
TERTIARY (external) constituencies*	General community system Legislatures—federal, state, regional, local Regulatory bodies Media		

*These are illustrative and not intended to be comprehensive.

The Elizabeth Blackwell Health Center for Women

The Elizabeth Blackwell Health Center for Women (referred to as Blackwell) is a feminist agency in Philadelphia whose mandate is to offer gynecological services to women. It was organized in the summer of 1974 by a group of women who saw a need for nonprofit, female-controlled services. They came together as a result of a common negative work experience in a commercially financed, physician-owned, for-profit abortion facility. It was clear to the founders that the quality of services provided to women is affected by the ownership, philosophy, and goals of the organization.

These women drew on the experience of other women around the country who were already involved in self-help clinics and study groups. They sought to apply what they knew of these experiences to their own goals and to their local context: a large city with an extensive, sophisticated, and fairly traditional medical care system.

The basic principles defining the mission of the organization reflected those articulated in feminist theory, as follows:

1. Health care is a right; the profit motive in health care can negatively affect quality of care.
2. Women have the right to understand their body functions and control their reproduction.
3. The needs of the consumer should be the utmost consideration in organizing the delivery of health care. . . . Consumers should be active participants in their personal health care and . . . participate in the decision-making activities of the health care system.
4. Health care should . . . emphasize maintenance of health and prevention of disease . . . and take into account physical, mental, social and environmental conditions. It should recognize female reproductive processes as health processes, not sickness.
5. A feminist working environment recognizes the value of every staff member's contribution, guarantees the right of every staff member to participate in decision making and encourages staff to expand their skills. (Blackwell Health Center for Women, 1975)

Guided by these principles, the founders organized a health center designed to provide high-quality, low-cost health services to women from all socioeconomic backgrounds.

Blackwell as a Social System

The Context

To understand the agency as a whole, with a systems view, the administrator must attend both to the contextual variables, as

27

discussed in Chapter 2, and to the variables within the organizational life space, as formulated by Slavin (1980). In brief, the contextual environment of Blackwell is exceedingly turbulent with constant change and shifts in all of the dimensions to be considered. Society's values and attitudes regarding birth control and abortion are not only in flux, but also in conflict with those of the agency. Great passion is expressed, and occasional violence is directed specifically against agencies such as this one.

The technology in the field is also changing: Not only are there new methods of birth control, but artificial insemination and surrogate parenting are two of the many dramatic technological developments that have a direct impact on Blackwell. The agency uses human resources—its staff, its board of directors, and its volunteers—in a new and creative way. Finally, every aspect is politicized, ranging from local demonstrations to federal legislation, which demands sophisticated political behavior on the part of the administrator.

Consequently, the assumptions that underlie the concept of administrative behavior as formulated in Chapter 1 are applicable here. The administrator has no choice but to be client-oriented and proactive and must empower the client-consumer, board of directors, and staff cohorts to become politically active as well.

Blackwell's Life Space

Blackwell uses Slavin's (1980) construct of organizational life space. Each of Slavin's three critical elements in all social service agencies—(1) the organization itself, (2) the provider of the service (the practitioner), and (3) the user (the client-consumer) of the service—plays a vital role.

In regard to the organization itself, the primary, internal constituency is the trustee system that includes the board of directors and its policy-making function. The founders of Blackwell made several critical decisions in this regard (Blackwell Health Center for Women, 1976). First, the board of directors would be elected by the consumers of the service and would be composed of interested individuals, primarily women, who would be representative of the women to be served (that is, by race, age, experience, and life-style). Second, the philosophies of self-help and participatory health care would inform its structure. Third, a system of checks and balances was designed to ensure the sharing of power in decision making. This was accomplished by requiring that one-third of the board of directors be staff-elected staff members and that all board committees of the board of directors include representatives of the Blackwell staff.

The secondary constituencies that are external to but directly involved with Blackwell play an important role. Of great importance is the connection with a network of feminist organizations in other areas of the country with whom the agency can discuss ideas and issues. The agency is also actively involved with a group of other feminist organizations in Philadelphia that offers interaction and support. Both networks have reduced Blackwell's sense of isolation and have provided support to both the board of directors and the staff. Simultaneously, these networks have helped to ensure that Blackwell stays in tune with the larger feminist movement.

Foundations are also an important secondary constituency for Blackwell, especially because the agency does not accept any government funding to ensure its autonomy and independence. Consequently, 20 percent of its funds come from foundation grants and private donations. The other 80 percent of its funds are generated through fees for the services rendered.

Several local coordinating bodies also play an important role. Womens Way, a Philadelphia fund-raising coalition of feminist organizations, is of particular importance because it serves as a conduit for private funds. Blackwell is also in constant communication, however, with Bread and Roses Community Fund and the Black United Fund of Pennsylvania, two other alternative organizations in Philadelphia.

A critical factor that must be taken into consideration concerns the self-sufficiency of the organization. The issue is whether the system is freestanding and autonomous or whether it is a part of a larger system, or a "host" setting, such as a social work department located in a hospital setting. The consequences of this fact have great significance in determining the administrator's degree of freedom. If the service is part of a larger organization, it shapes the dimensions of the system that the social work administrator must handle. Because Blackwell is freestanding, the administrator and the board of directors can be in total control of the service, in contrast to a social service department in a hospital setting, which would be constrained because of its association with a hospital.

According to Slavin's (1980) formulation, the administrator must also deal with the external tertiary constituencies. These are powerful influences on Blackwell. Federal and state abortion legislation has a direct impact on the agency, as does the "right-to-life" movement, which has become increasingly active in its organized opposition to agencies that offer women abortions and counseling on whether to have an abortion. In addition, the news media are a critical tertiary element with which continuous and active contact is required.

Theoretical Perspectives

In regard to service providers, the second element identified in Slavin's organizational life space, Blackwell presents a complicated picture because it employs a diverse group of workers. This primary constituency consists of nonprofessionals, volunteers, social workers, physicians, and student interns. Thus, it employs people with a broad array of both sociological and educational backgrounds. The administrator must be cognizant of the diverse values, orientations, skills, experiences, interests, and needs of these different groups.

Much creative thinking has gone into the area of staff utilization to ensure an equalitarian and participatory environment. In addition to the staff's participation on the board of directors, in the early years of the agency's existence, there was considerable flexibility and job rotation, although each staff member had a specific job description. This was done to equalize the status of all staff members, regardless of their professional or nonprofessional background. As the organization matured and the staff grew in number, staff members were less likely to carry responsibilities or perform tasks that were unrelated to their own jobs. Staff still relate to each other as peers, however, despite differences in salaries, job titles, and responsibilities.

An interesting mechanism exists to protect this equalitarian relationship. Hiring and firing of all staff except the executive director are the responsibility of a committee composed of Blackwell staff whose membership is rotated among the entire staff on a quarterly basis. This committee also decides on the salaries to be paid to new staff members, within ranges set by a committee of the board of directors. In addition, all staff members are evaluated annually by all the others. An unsatisfactory evaluation or performance poor enough to question continuation of the employee is brought before the staff committee for formal review and determination. Staff members have been put on probation or have been fired by this committee in a process that is both lengthy and, at times, painful.

A broad array of secondary constituencies reflects the diversity of staff composition in the form of numerous professional associations and interest groups. The tertiary constituencies are basically those described above in the discussion of the organization itself.

The third important element in the system are the clients or consumers. In Blackwell the decision was made to call the women to be served "consumers," to enhance their power in their relationships with the service providers at the center, in contrast to the connotation of powerlessness inherent in the terms "patient" or "client."

Blackwell's services have developed and broadened to reflect the needs of women of all ages and at all stages of life. From the outset it has offered well-woman gynecological care, including contraception, pregnancy testing, options counseling, abortion services, and health education (for example, workshops on self-help and consumer rights and presentations on a variety of health issues). In addition, Blackwell has always provided gynecological care for women past childbearing age.

Currently, more than a decade after its founding, Blackwell's services include full maternity care, with an out-of-hospital birth center staffed by certified nurse-midwives; artificial insemination for fertile women; and educational programs on menopause, hysterectomy, fertility awareness, nutrition, and childbearing options.

The responsiveness to a broad spectrum of women is assured by the operating principle that "staff and Board would be representative of the women who were to be served (i.e., race, age, experience and lifestyle) and would provide services they themselves would wish to use" (Blackwell Health Center for Women, 1975, p. 2).

Secondary constituencies of the consumers include midwife associations, other professional associations that have expertise in the services offered, and other special interest groups concerned about artificial insemination programs, such as gay and lesbian organizations. As discussed above, other feminist organizations, both at the local and national levels, are of critical importance. Not only do they provide support but they also serve to stimulate new programs and services. The experiences of an agency in another part of the country that provides new services and experimental programs often help Blackwell to broaden its approach if it is appropriate for the consumers in the area it serves.

Understanding the Whole

The complexity of the social service agency as a social system is evident, because it includes external and internal elements and primary, secondary, and tertiary constituencies. It must be emphasized that one's position within the organization determines one's vantage point and perspective. Thus, a consumer will view Blackwell from her service needs and experiences; a board member will be mission oriented and concerned with the development and use of organizational resources to meet organizational goals; and staff members will focus on their specific work responsibilities, agency policies, and salary and benefits issues. It is the agency administrator who must be aware of and responsive to all these aspects of the organization.

MAKING THE SHIFT

Dramatic changes are necessary in making the shift from direct practice to administration. There are no easy answers to be provided

31

or zodiac signs to be read when making the decision of whether to shift from direct practice to administration. Perhaps the most important indicators are the individual's gut reactions to the ideas presented in this volume.

This chapter has identified an array of different perspectives and behaviors implicit in administration both from a personal and systems vantage point. The following questions may help the reader to understand these perspectives and behaviors: Are they of interest to you? Do they intrigue you? Are you stimulated to think about the questions that have been raised and the issues that have been identified? Are you challenged to use your knowledge of direct practice and client needs in a different manner? Do you want to develop a totally different set of professional skills and approaches?

One student specializing in social work administration questioned whether he was suited for administration because he did not have an active style or charismatic personality. He was responding to a stereotype of the aggressive executive, but there are different needs for different leadership styles and approaches, and not every administrator is a charismatic leader. Much depends on the particular organizational requisites. The challenge is to understand the system and to be able to assess creatively the appropriate leadership approach for that setting at that point in the agency's development.

Some administrators excel in some areas; others excel in other areas. The trick is to "know thyself" and to assess the particular position to determine whether the position is appropriate in terms of individual interests, skills, and experiences. It should also be noted that administrators do not have to do everything themselves; they do some things themselves, whereas other assignments can be delegated to others. The bottom line is only that the task be done effectively, because the administrator is responsible for the total operation.

There is no one route to travel for a meaningful career in social work: There are, indeed, "different strokes for different folks." Every productive participant in the social service agency makes an important contribution. The challenge is to determine the level at which one wishes to work and then to broaden one's knowledge and skills to perform that job effectively.

4

A Theoretical Model of Social Service Agency Development

A critical function for social work administration is planning for change to make possible in the future that which has not yet occurred in the present. In Selznick's (1957) view, the zenith of administration is the vision for the future, a characteristic essential for transforming the competent but unexceptional administrator into the ideal institutional leader.

An orientation toward change and a vision for the future, however, are necessary but are insufficient for effective leadership. They must be closely linked to an analysis of the particular social service agency, its past, and its present. This chapter presents a model of social service agency development that serves as an instrument for planning agency change. The model was conceptualized as a result of a study of 22 social service agencies (Perlmutter, 1969), and this chapter is a revision of that report.

The social work literature has shown little interest in the concepts of life cycles and developmental stages of organizations. Yet, as Patti (1983) suggests, an understanding of the stages of organizational development and the goals and characteristics of each stage has important implications for managerial behavior.

Selznick's (1957) discussion of leadership is based on a developmental notion of organizational life. He focuses on a

> natural-history approach which can call attention to the developmental problems that arise in organizational experience. . . . To the extent that similar situations summon like responses from similar groups, we may expect to find organizational evolutionary patterns. The hope is that this uniformity, once discovered, may provide tools for more adequate description and more perceptive diagnosis. (p. 103)

Theoretical Perspectives

As noted in Chapter 1, theory is important because it provides a handle for understanding and action. The following discussion presents one theoretical model and illustrates its applications to agency realities.

THEORETICAL MODEL

Three developmental stages can be identified in the life of a social agency: self-interest, professionalism, and social interest. Stage 1, self-interest, is the initial organizational phase when, in response to pressing social problems, the social service agency is organized. Stage 2, professionalism, occurs when the urgency has abated and the agency can focus on refining its services. Stage 3, social interest, is the response to new social problems that are directly related to those that led to the original formation of the agency. Although this model is intended to explain the workings of a total social service agency, Patti (1983) has also found it useful when applied to the development of a specific program within the social service agency.

An orderly progression of growth is implicit in the proposed model. Stage 1 must be achieved before stage 2 can occur, and stage 3 can only follow stage 2. Although a relatively young agency may be in the second stage in relation to its professional sophistication, a careful study of its early history will reveal evidence of the first stage, self-interest, even though it may have been of short duration. As is the case with a public agency, on the other hand, the first stage occurs before the legislation, or social policy, that creates the agency. This first stage is crucial because the groundwork is laid in the community for the recognition of the problem and the acceptance of this function as a public responsibility to be supported by public funds. An agency that moves prematurely to a subsequent stage will not be grounded firmly in its operation or its public sanction.

This model takes into account all elements of the system, both internal and external. Before each stage of development is discussed in greater detail, the following eight elements, or variables, that have been selected to provide an understanding of the social service agency as a social system are presented: (1) external socioeconomic conditions, (2) value system, (3) institutional mission, (4) administrative leadership, (5) structure of authority, (6) clients system, (7) agency services, and (8) intersystem relationships.

It should be noted that three of these variables are central in shaping the agency's development: (1) the changing external environment (which the agency cannot control), (2) the value system (which the agency can control), and (3) the definition of institutional mission (which the agency can control). The intersection of these three elements, or independent variables, unfolds in the choices and decisions made by the administrator about the remaining variables. The administrative response can lead to failure, survival, or success, and careful attention to the model's variables paves the way for a successful course of events.

The eight variables are briefly described below and serve as the basis for the examination of a particular agency at each stage of development.

Although external socioeconomic conditions are not part of the internal agency system, an analysis of changing historical circumstances is essential to an understanding of the agency at each stage of development. The initial motivation to organize a voluntary social service agency is determined by these external conditions; the movement through the stages can be understood only in relation to the external conditions.

The value system of an agency is operative from the earliest, embryonic phase of the formation of an agency and serves to set the overall framework for all the other variables. Although agency values coincide in part with those of the broader society, in the case of the voluntary social service agency, they may be either disparate or more specialized in a particular sphere. Because values are most enduring and least susceptible to change (Parsons, 1961), the ideology of the organization remains relevant throughout its entire life cycle; the emphasis placed on specific values within that overall philosophy varies according to the specific stage of development.

Selznick (1957) defines *institutional mission* as "the setting of goals . . . as a creative task. It entails a self assessment to discover the true commitments of the organization, as set by effective internal and external demands" (p. 62). This is a critical process in the development of the social service agency and is the intersection of values with governance and agency policy.

Administrative leadership must be responsive to the organization's particular needs at each stage of development. The selection of an administrator should take this into account to ensure a better match between the agency and its leader. For example, a charismatic leader is needed to negotiate successfully in the volatile external environment that sets the stage for the shift to the third stage of social interest, in contrast to the more professionally and organizationally exacting leadership required in the second stage of professionalism.

The structure of authority, whether it is centralized or decentralized, is an important element and should be designed to take into account the life-cycle stage of organizational development. From an initial centralized arrangement, as the agency becomes more professional, a decentralized structure would be expected to develop.

The client system must be examined to analyze the evolutionary development of the agency. Whom does the agency serve? Does the client group change as the agency moves from self-interest to social interest?

Agency services are an important variable because they embody and implement the values of the organization. An analysis of these concrete operations will shed light on the attainment of, or the failure to attain, each stage of development.

Intersystem relationships is that aspect of the agency that relates to the larger society. Do outside relationships exist? Are these relationships compatible with the value framework? Do the relationships change with the developmental stages? This dimension focuses on the boundaries of the agency and tests its ability to work with other social service agencies and organizations in the community.

THE THREE STAGES OF DEVELOPMENT

Stage 1: Self-Interest

A variety of unsolved social problems stimulates the creation of voluntary social service agencies when the treatment of these problems appears to be possible and pressing. An ideology is made explicit as the initial formalization process occurs. Within the framework of broad societal values, such as equal opportunity for all and minimal federal government activity, more cogent values are selected in regard to social welfare, such as the alleviation of poverty and the focus on individual adjustment. To mobilize sufficient support for the formation of a new agency, this ideology must be broad enough to enlist the support of both a power structure—the board of directors—and a staff to carry out the agency's mandate.

In this initial stage of development, the institutional mission is defined. It links the social problem and the ideology with the particular system's identity as its goals and policies are defined. A sectarian family agency, for example, differs from a nonsectarian family agency. Although the social problems that both agencies address may be the same, the institutional mission of the sectarian agency encompasses particular values that are relevant to the identity of its auspices.

In the first stage of development, these first three variables—(1) social problem, (2) value system, and (3) institutional mission—may produce the élan of a social movement, especially when a subgroup of society that is not accorded equal treatment is involved and takes the situation into its own hands (Wirth, 1957). The recent organization of agencies to serve victims of acquired immune deficiency syndrome is an example of agencies at the self-interest stage of development.

In regard to administrative leadership, the administrator must work closely with the board of directors to implement its intent. This is not the time to exercise dramatic professional initiatives. It should be noted that middle management is least defined in stage 1 because its function depends on the more developed bureaucratic apparatus of the subsequent stages. At those later times, the administrator and professional staff will move into more ascendant positions.

The client group during the period of self-interest is carefully defined as the victim of the circumstance that stimulated the agency's formation. The services in the self-interest period, therefore, are directly relevant to the original social problem. The emphasis is on getting help to as many people as possible (that is, quantity). Services are oriented toward the ends to be gained, and less attention is given to the means of achieving them (that is, quality).

Relationships between the social service agency and other organizations in the larger system are rather limited at this time, and the new agency relates primarily to other agencies with similar ideologies and missions. Furthermore, it is not selected for contact by dissimilar organizations, because established agencies tend to relate to others in the established agency network (Levine & White, 1961).

Stage 2: Professionalism

The shift from stage 1 to stage 2 results from new external conditions that affect the agency. At stage 2, the social problems that stimulated stage 1 have been either resolved or reduced in urgency. Consequently, all the variables in stage 2 operate in a different social context.

In this new context, the basic and distinctive character of the agency is not questioned; the ideology and the institutional mission of the agency are generally maintained, but a new dimension is introduced. Whereas the initial stage focused on meeting the needs of as many people as possible, the shift to professionalism involves a focus on quality of service, creating an internal rather than an external orientation.

New patterns of authority evolve, and the structure is decentralized to grant authority to the professional worker. Richan (1961) observes: "The 'pure' professional is controlled . . . by a generalized body of knowledge and generalized skills assimilated over an extended training period. Thus, the worker can apply his knowledge to a greater variety of situations than is possible under concrete instructions, and can use himself more flexibly" (p. 23). The professional (that is, both the administrator and middle management) is therefore relatively independent of the board of directors in the transactions of agency business. As the professional moves into ascendancy and as the board of directors becomes more passive in its role, there is a shift toward an emphasis on techniques and standards and away from the original institutional mission of the agency, which, in this stage of development, is in danger of becoming somewhat distorted. This is a risk that often results from professionalism and has been noted in the organizational literature (Sills, 1957).

Services are refined and improved as the worker-client contact becomes both more extensive in terms of the number of contacts and intensive in terms of the nature of the services rendered. Directly related to the emphasis on quality is a redefinition of the client group. Although in stage 2 the definition of the broad characteristics of the client group remains the same as it was in stage 1, the group can now be refined into its constituent parts so that they can receive more intensive professional services. A broad group, for example, chemically addicted individuals, can be divided into various subgroups (for example, employed adults or teenagers), with special services designed and tailored for each group. This emphasis on intensive service to clients results in a focus of attention on the agency's means rather than on its ends.

The investment in professionalism is ultimately realized as new relationships develop between the agency and other organizations in the system. During stage 2 much more interaction takes place with other professional agencies that share expertise and interests.

Stage 3: Social Interest

To understand the shift from stage 2 to stage 3, it is again important to examine external conditions. A prerequisite to the shift is the emergence of a new social problem that is related to the problem that stimulated the initial formation of the agency but that involves basic divergences. The redefinition of mission is not a clear-cut matter; the very existence of the new social problem requires the agency to reassess its position in relation to the broader community. By moving from an insular position of self-interest to a broader professional stance, the agency has come into contact with the larger social system, if only in the professional context. At this stage of development the agency has not only experienced success in its own performance but has also achieved a position of status within the broader network of professional agencies. It can therefore reexamine its value framework from a position of strength.

Although the agency maintains its basic integrity throughout the developmental process, as discussed earlier, the interpretation and emphasis placed on values vary by stage. The redefinition of mission that is necessary to move to stage 3 occurs within the broad limits of the basic ideology of the system by emphasizing less firmly grounded, precarious values rather than acceptable, secure values (Clark, 1956). A family service agency, for example, that has provided only counseling may move to broaden its repertoire of services to include "hard" services, such as housing and employment. The effective shift to the stage of social interest, however, requires not only that the professional staff be ready to welcome the new populations, but also that the board of directors have the same priorities. All parts of the agency system must be involved.

Thus, in regard to governance, the board is again actively involved in policy decisions, in contrast to stage 2, when the executive director and the professional staff were dominant. The members of the board of directors and administration must engage in serious ideological discussions to prepare for the policy decisions that may change the character of the agency. An élan reminiscent of stage 1 becomes evident at stage 3, but it is now the joint endeavor of the board of directors and the administration. A more complete and functionally differentiated agency can emerge with greater independence and flexibility.

Agency services also reflect the new stage of social interest, because there is a merger of quality with quantity. Although the value of professional competence is retained, the thrust for delivery of service to meet the new pressing problem assumes importance. Flexibility and experimentation are essential in effecting the newly defined priorities. The overall orientation is on both means and ends, as opposed to the stress on ends in the first stage and on means in the second stage.

In stage 3, the client group is qualitatively different from that of the first two stages and is directly related to the new social problem. Although the initial client group continues to be important, the shift to the social interest stage requires a broader target population. In stage 3, the agency seeks to serve not only those who are affected by the original social problem, but also those who are experiencing the new one.

A change in intersystem activity becomes evident at the social interest stage as the agency moves from its internal orientation to an external one. A much broader spectrum of relationships develops. Whereas in stage 1 the agency establishes relationships with similar agencies concerned with the same social problem and in stage 2 it establishes relationships with agencies that address other professional services, in stage 3 new paths of interaction emerge. Contacts develop with a variety of organizations, both professional and non-professional, as programs evolve in relation to the new social problem. The effect is felt in the broader community as well.

IMPLICATIONS OF THE MODEL

It is most fruitful to approach a study of organizations from an evolutionary point of view, examining them not merely for what they are but also for what they are in the process of becoming. A consideration of the specific variables of the system clarifies the limitations and potential for organizational change.

The model encourages specific recognition of the system's part in facilitating the developmental process. The recruitment of professional elites, for instance, can be more specifically related to a newly defined mission. Similarly, the administrator can assess the position of the agency more effectively in regard to its external commitments.

The developmental model described here also allows for recognition of the importance of the ideological framework in developing more effective agency strategies. In seeking to guard the secure values of the original mission of the agency while nurturing the precarious values of the newly defined one, restructuring the agency—for example, into two parts—can be a technique for meeting a variety of new commitments while simultaneously honoring the old ones.

An orderly progression of growth is implicit in this theoretical model of agency development, and vestiges of previous stages must be taken into account; even a radical shift of emphasis does not eliminate the earlier developmental history. Stage 1 is, therefore, crucial for the initial self-definition of the organization because it clarifies its goals and orders its commitments. It provides justification for the position that services for African Americans, for example, must be developed by and for the African American community itself. Clearly, self-interest must come first.

Agencies must pay attention to the changing external conditions to remain relevant; this demands a flexibility and an ever-present readiness to redefine the agency's mission. The Woman's Christian Temperance Union is an example of a one-dimensional organization vis-à-vis its organizational mission (Gusfield, 1955). At the time that external circumstances changed with the end of Prohibition, the organization lacked professional leadership to shift from self-interest to professionalism. Because the governing body was composed solely of lay members imbued with the social movement orientation of stage 1, the organization remained fixated at the self-interest level and eventually became irrelevant.

It should be noted that a common trait among all agencies is the tendency to be internally directed and technique oriented. This leads to a potential fixation at stage 2, professionalism. This can be illustrated by an example from the field.

The ABC Jewish Vocational Service (not its real name) was in stage 2 of development, professionalism. The agency obtained public funds for the development of a project from the Vocational Rehabilitation Administration and the National Institute of Mental Health, both of which are federal agencies concerned with technical and professional advances. The project they supported was compatible with the original mission of the agency. The receipt of additional funds from the Office of Economic Opportunity precipitated a crisis situation in the agency, however, because the Office of Economic Opportunity objectives require a broad social commitment to serve new client groups. This commitment was appropriate for stage 3, the social interest stage of agency development, a stage that it had not yet reached.

The administrator, in this case, had not done his homework. The agency had not reexamined its mission, given the change in external circumstances. The administrator had set policy unilaterally by writing the proposal and obtaining the funds. The agency value system and its governing board of directors were still at stage 2, however, and were not ready to shift to stage 3. The board of directors precipitously ended the project and returned the funds.

The crisis for the organization and the negative consequences it faced in the community can be imagined. The outcome might have been different had the administrator used this theoretical model of social service agency development as a basis for organizational analysis and as a guide for his actions. The model might have helped him to recognize that the board of directors was not yet ready to broaden the agency's mission.

Theoretical Perspectives

This three-stage model describes one successful course of events that can result from careful attention to the model and its variables. An agency may well be effective in meeting social needs without progressing through all three stages, but the administrator and the board of directors should be aware of the choices they are making and the costs and benefits of remaining in one of the first two stages. In other words, this model is both descriptive and prescriptive. It offers one possible route to success: Chapter 5 presents a case study of an agency that successfully went through the three stages of development. Given the centrality of organizational mission in the developmental process, the discussion in Chapter 5 is organized around this variable.

Part II Administrative Practice
Perspectives

5

A Case Study of Successful Agency Change

This above all: to thine own self be true.

—Hamlet (act 1, scene 3, line 78)

The struggle of individuals to determine who they are and how they wish to shape their lives also exists for those who work in any social service agency. What is the fundamental purpose of the agency? What was the problem that brought it into existence? What does this mean for its present activity and future directions?

It is common for an organization to get so involved in its present interest, activities, priorities, and commitments that its guiding mission is overlooked. This is not unique to the social service sector; in fact, much of the organizational development consultation provided to businesses and industries centers on helping those systems trace their fundamental raison d'être. As Drucker (1973) explains in *Management: Tasks • Responsibilities • Practices,*

> Only a clear definition of the mission and purpose of the business makes possible clear and realistic business objectives. It is the foundation for the priorities, strategies, plans, and work assignments. It is the starting point for the design of managerial jobs and, above all, for the design of managerial structures. Structure follows strategy. (p. 75)

Selznick's (1957) work is also useful because he calls attention to the importance of understanding the purpose of the organization as fundamental for any discussion of administration. His use of the term "institutional mission" includes the setting of organizational goals in relation to the "true commitments of the organization as set by effective internal and external demands" (p. 62).

An understanding of organizational mission is central not only for the understanding of organizations but also for the application of the theoretical model of social service agency development. This chapter uses case material to illustrate the applicability of this developmental model. Again it is emphasized that it is necessary to understand the environmental context and the value system as the preconditions for the determination of the central purpose of the organization and its organizational mission.

A CASE STUDY: THE JEWISH EMPLOYMENT AND VOCATIONAL SERVICE

The Jewish Employment and Vocational Service (JEVS) has been deliberately selected for use as a case study because it is a microcosm of the broader social welfare community in its involvement with central contemporary social welfare issues. The agency is in the voluntary sector under the aegis of a voluntary board of directors; it is part of the social service agency network at the local level; and its sectarian nature calls attention to the major dilemmas and possibilities faced by any special interest agency, whether it is oriented to ethnicity, religion, sexual preference, or any other unique target population characteristic. Finally, it illustrates the changing nature of the voluntary sector because this sector has become increasingly dependent on public funding (Perlmutter, 1969).

JEVS is located in a major urban area. The basic function of this agency is to help individuals find jobs; the vocational counseling and testing services rest on the assumption that work is the client's ultimate goal.

Of central interest in this discussion are the following questions: Has JEVS retained its unique identity and character in the 50 years of its existence or has it shifted with the times? Have external pressures and resources (that is, the availability of government funds and priorities) shaped the organization's development and shifted its mission, or has the agency as a social system shaped its own destiny, within the realities of a changing environment?

JEVS and Stage 1: Self-interest

In stage 1 of its organizational development, every social service agency responds to a particular problem in the environment; the response reflects its ideological value orientations. In JEVS several streams of influence were active. The enormous economic dislocations of the Great Depression in the 1930s, which affected all groups in American society, had unique implications for the Jewish community. Not only was anti-Semitism rampant until World War II, preventing Jews from entering major areas of employment, but the influx of refugees from Europe also stimulated the Jewish community to establish its own programs to meet its special needs.

Two basic values informed this new social service agency. The first, which it shared with the broader American society, viewed work as a fundamental expectation of all the citizenry; keeping the able-bodied poor off the dole was a basic value and objective accepted by JEVS (1947):

> We have proved to our own satisfaction, at least, that we have saved the community more money by removing people from relief rolls, or keeping them off, than it has cost to operate the Bureau. (p. 1)

The second value was the Jewish view of charity that not only assumes the responsibility of caring for its own but also views it as most virtuous. Thus, the definition of institutional mission established the unique identity of JEVS by linking the social problem with the ideology. This is evident in the Articles of Incorporation (JEVS, 1941), which marked the formal beginnings of the organization:

> The purposes for which the corporation is founded are: (a) To provide facilities for scientific and practical adjustment of people to jobs, (b) To provide facilities for a better understanding of the job seekers' abilities and personal characteristics, (c) To learn of the employment opportunities . . . , (d) To find all the community resources where suitable training can be secured, and (e) To provide and seek opportunities for the placement of job seekers.

The minutes of the first meeting of the board of directors further specified that the agency was unique because no fees were charged and the clients were Jewish.

The agency's sectarian identity is critical in this developmental analysis. Ensuring the agency's Jewish identity serves as a vital indicator of the agency's ability to protect its autonomy and to set its own priorities. This issue consequently affected many aspects of decision making in the support of its unique institutional mission. For example, the agency had to decide whether to be open on Saturday, the Jewish Sabbath, to serve employers. The agency had to decide whether non-Jews should serve on the board of directors or its committees.

The agency also had to decide whether its name should be changed from "The Employment and Vocational Bureau," its original title, to include the designation "Jewish."

Although a fairly clear-cut policy emerged in most areas concerning Jewishness as being central to the institutional mission, some ambivalence was also evident. A positive sense of Jewish values guided the following two decisions: (1) the bureau would not be open on the Sabbath and (2) non-Jewish members could not serve on the agency's board of directors but would be invited to join the Employer Contact Committee "on the basis of their future value in breaking down anti-Jewish discrimination" (JEVS, 1942). It is important to note, however, that the name Jewish Employment Service was rejected in this first stage; it seems that at that time the board of directors was unwilling to identify publicly the sectarian nature of the agency, although it clearly defined the population to be served as Jewish only.

Changes in the environment during stage 1 put pressure on the agency to make some changes that could be viewed as a threat to its original mission. In 1945, when World War II had ended, "the matter of accepting non-Jewish war veterans was . . . brought up for discussion. . . . It was agreed that non-Jewish war veterans should not be turned away" (JEVS, 1945).

This was a critical decision that was to affect the long-range identity of the agency; from that time on JEVS did not refuse to serve non-Jews. The decision galvanized the board of directors into making its priorities clear, however. In 1951 the board voted to change the agency name to The Jewish Employment and Vocational Service, a step it was not ready to take, or did not need to take, when its clientele was 100 percent Jewish.

As predicted by the model, the primary focus in stage 1 was on delivery of service to as many people as possible, at the expense of attention to the quality and techniques of service delivery.

Although the complex social problems of the postwar period demanded extensive time for individual counseling, the Federation of Jewish Agencies (the central planning and funding body of the Jewish community, comparable with the United Way) put increasing pressure on the agency to focus on placements, not counseling.

> The trend toward reducing the number of counseling interviews is in the right direction. Efforts should be made to curtail the number of interviews still further. The goal should be to attain an average of four counseling interviews with the applicant. . . .

> Budgetary and personnel limitations require that emphasis be placed on specific vocational guidance . . . and that directive rather than non-directive techniques be employed. (Goldberg & Maddow, 1948, p. 82)

Although this policy appeared to be dysfunctional to the agency in the short run and was instituted in violation of the integrity of the system, in the long run it played a positive and essential role. Through the internal instability that it created, it paved the way for the shift to stage 2, the professional stage of development.

JEVS and Stage 2: Professionalism

The actual event that served to stimulate the developmental shift of the agency to the second stage of development was an external one, as suggested by the theoretical model. The Federation of Jewish Agencies expressed dissatisfaction with the allocation of JEVS's resources because it had not met its community-based campaign goal:

> The consolidation of services [was necessary] rather than the expansion of any particular program; and . . . the values of the vocational service appeared to community leaders (and Federation) to be less significant over the long future than those of other community services. (JEVS, 1954)

A crisis in JEVS was thus precipitated by the Federation's clear statement concerning the low priority it accorded JEVS; the very existence of the agency seemed to be at stake. This was coupled with the Federation's attempt to restrict the agency's mission to placement, at the expense of the counseling function, as discussed above. The board of directors' response to this crisis would determine the agency's future existence.

The unanticipated consequence of these events was that the board of directors was stimulated to strengthen the agency's autonomy. To accomplish this, the board recognized its dependence on the professionals and their unique role in the quest to improve the caliber of service. Fortunately, at that time a new force emerged in the broader society germane to the agency and potentially supportive of its needs. The federal Vocational Rehabilitation Act of 1954 revolutionized relationships between the public sector and the voluntary, nonprofit agencies through the provision of grants for special projects. Thus, the social conditions in the external environment nurtured stage 2.

Administrative Practice Perspectives

Attention moved from external social problems to a focus on standards and techniques. This was not an automatic response to the external conditions; rather, the professionals who were held in abeyance and could not express their priorities in the earlier self-interest period were able to assert their expertise.

The shift to stage 2, professionalism, did not entail a change in ideology: the basic values that informed the original founding of the agency were still extant, albeit with different priorities. Still operative were the importance of the work ethic, JEVS's status as a voluntary agency, and JEVS's commitment to sectarianism; what became emphasized was a focus on quality service.

The board of directors demonstrated a new clarity of agency identity and mission when it decided to design a strategy that would protect JEVS's interests. The executive director made the board of directors aware of the new program possibilities with government funds. Before approaching the Federation about using funds from outside sources, the board developed a strategy that would put it in the driver's seat in regard to agency operations. The board aimed to validate the need for a new program and to prove the agency's competency in running it. The board set the stage by requesting that the Federation of Jewish Agencies participate "in a study of the agency's objectives, program, practices, and accomplishments" (JEVS, 1955). As a result, the Federation allocated funds for a 1-year period, which gave the agency ample time to develop a new service in the form of a sheltered workshop and to use it as a base for the development of future projects with government funds.

Although the proposal for a sheltered workshop appeared to be a routine professional decision, it was, in fact, a critical decision that had long-term consequences for the organization. Not only was the local Health and Welfare Council invited to become involved in the agency's planning process, and thus, for the first time, bring to bear the broader professional community perspective, but a new external resource, that of government funds, was also developed.

Again, it must be emphasized that the decision to take public funds was made by the agency from a position of strength and clarity regarding its institutional mission of quality professional service, but it was not made easily. The board of directors debated the issue for almost the entire decade of the 1950s. It ultimately agreed with the professionals, however, that the quality of agency service would distinctly benefit from government financing, particularly in the larger ratio of professional staff to clients. "The income received from this source offers a financial benefit not only to the workshop but also to the general agency" (JEVS, 1958a).

The central dilemma for JEVS as a result of this decision concerned its sectarian identity, because a nonsectarian policy was required for the acceptance of public funds. Two areas of primary concern existed. The first concern was whether the Jewish community would continue to have its special needs met. The second concern was how the agency would relate to the Federation. These issues were clearly defined and handled.

The needs of the Jewish community would be met because the new programs would be planned around those needs, such as "a workshop rehabilitation program for older disabled workers . . . and for the vocational rehabilitation of the chronically ill" (JEVS, 1960). Clearly, a greater number of people in the Jewish community could be given workshop services in the long run than could be achieved by Federation funds alone. Thus, the needs of the larger society and the Jewish community could be met simultaneously.

At no time did JEVS consider severing its ties with the Federation of Jewish Agencies, regardless of the availability of public funds. To the contrary, in its desire to remain part of the Jewish social welfare community, JEVS sought to cement this relationship.

> The Board reviewed in detail the implications to the agency of operating a government financed project at the workshop. It formally approved the recommendations . . . that the government grant be accepted and that the proposed program be instituted. It was suggested that representatives of the Board meet with Federation to interpret the benefits accruing to the community by accepting the government financing of the workshop and to clarify that the government grant was contingent upon the continued support by Federation of the present workshop which constituted the necessary matching by the agency of money at the rate of $1.00 by JEVS for each $2.00 provided by OVR [Office of Vocational Rehabilitation]. The Board established its position in accepting the federal funds on the ground that the project would add to the number of Jewish clients served in the community without affecting the policy of the workshop and the commitment to Federation that had been originally made. (JEVS, 1958b)

It should be noted, however, that because the quality of service became of primary interest, the professional staff was less concerned with the sectarian identity of their clients than it was with their particular service needs. As a result, the government's requirement of nonsectarianism was not viewed as inappropriate by the professional staff, which was the dominant decision-making group at that stage of development. Their priorities were professional, in contrast to the board's priorities regarding the agency's special responsibility to sectarianism.

An administrative strategy was developed whereby the "core" JEVS agency, financed by Jewish communal funds, served the Jewish community primarily; in contradistinction, the workshop, which was mainly subsidized by government fees and contracts, had a completely nonsectarian intake. Thus, in the core JEVS agency, 80 percent of the clients were Jewish compared with 1 percent in the workshop.

JEVS moved into stage 2 of its organizational development, professionalism, with a clear sense of its unique identity, autonomy, and clarity of mission. It used its external resources effectively to meet its short-term objectives and, ultimately, to ensure a stable and ongoing agency.

JEVS and Stage 3: Social Interest

The 1960s was a period of broad unrest—many people were dissatisfied with American society. Poor people were increasingly angry with the inequitable distribution of resources; the nonwhite population was outraged with discrimination and the lack of equal opportunity; urban dwellers were increasingly aware of unresolved social problems. Although the problems of poverty and unemployment were in the same broad arena as the initial problems that stimulated the formation of JEVS, the Jewish community was no longer the population at risk; the major group in need of services related to employment was the African American population.

The agency had a clear choice: It could remain at stage 2 of development, professionalism, with service to the non-Jewish population being incidental to its professional thrust, or it could focus on the new social realities and, by a redefinition of its mission, move past its own communal needs to a new external orientation toward the broader non-Jewish population.

The values that informed the formation of the agency and its move to professionalism were still vital. The problems were similar to those of the self-interest period (stage 1) and the work ethic remained an important focus. The traditional Jewish concern with the plight of the poor was extended to include the non-Jewish urban poor. Although high professional standards were still valued, they no longer dominated the agency's mission; of equal importance was the plight of the new target population and the need to provide services to them.

Stage 3 of development was precipitated by the board of directors' dissatisfaction with the sudden growth of the agency and its allocation of facilities. Professionalism had brought with it an extensive variety of programs under both public and sectarian funds:

> A review is necessary regarding the use of public money and the core agency's responsibility to the Jewish community. It might be necessary to introduce services to narrow segments of society in order to meet financial requirements (e.g. whereas school dropouts are a problem in the Jewish community, we may require services for juvenile delinquency for which money is available). Implicit in this problem is the question of Jewish community service and how it is reconciled with services to large numbers of non-Jews. The Board needs to study the question of agency direction and growth. (JEVS, 1962)

This discussion illustrates the conscious and deliberate process of redefinition of agency mission that characterized the development of JEVS throughout the next 5-year period. Agency documents of this period record the constant preoccupation with this issue by all committees of the board of directors. The board's careful formulation of its new directions supports the theoretical model described here, because it designed a deliberate and carefully planned response to the external stimulus of public funds.

The board of directors and the executive director devised an effective strategy by which the seemingly disparate goals of serving the sectarian versus the broader, nonsectarian community were reconciled. The primary responsibility of the agency in the provision of ongoing services was to the Jewish community, whose planning and funding mechanisms were retained by the Jewish community through the Federation of Jewish Agencies. The broader, nonsectarian community would be served through special programs developed on a short-term, experimental basis and financed by public funds.

An important consequence of this position was the development of a project by JEVS whose target population was completely non-Jewish: an employment project for youths who had dropped out of school that was funded by the U.S. Department of Labor. Clearly, the agency could not operate the massive programs that would be necessary to meet the total community's needs; it could, however, share its knowledge with others to help broaden the scope of professional programs in the community through research, demonstration, and consultation.

The success of the agency in obtaining government contracts created another tension that was directly related to the issue of autonomy and clarity of mission. In a 4-year period, the amount of public funding quadrupled from $150,000 to $674,520, whereas the contribution from the Federation of Jewish Agencies remained stable. It was very seductive to have large sums of money available for programs designed by the professional staff; at that time the agency could easily have been coopted by the government to serve only the general public. In fact, this did happen to a JEVS in another metropolitan area, which left the sectarian fold, dropped the designation of Jewish from its name, and became a nonsectarian employment and vocational service.

The JEVS in this case study was intent on setting its own goals, however. The availability of government funds would not change its direction. Although the route was not an unambivalent one, each debate strengthened the view that sectarian funding had to be used in every agency program that received public funds to ensure that government policies would not completely govern the program.

A new strategy was developed to meet the enormous growth of the agency through public funds. The structural decentralization of the agency was attempted with the establishment of a nonsectarian subsidiary, the Vocational Research Institute, as a nonprofit corporation. Although the primary objective was to facilitate the receipt of public grants on the theory that a nonsectarian entity would be more attractive to the government, other objectives included involving the total community in creating the policies of these nonsectarian programs and improving the agency's image in the community. In reality, the Vocational Research Institute never got off the ground because the government wanted to do business directly with JEVS, the respected and established organization.

The external orientation implicit in the social interest stage was clear as JEVS became involved with a much broader community of nonsectarian and government agencies, adding to the sectarian ones of the self-interest period (stage 1) and to the professional ones of stage 2. The JEVS experience helped to stimulate the Federation of Jewish Agencies into developing a policy on the involvement of Federation and the sectarian agencies within its orbit in the broader community within the context of change.

IMPLICATIONS OF THIS CASE STUDY

Its institutional mission is the bedrock of a social service agency because it continuously sets the boundaries of, and the conditions for, the agency's response to the community's needs. This is of prime importance, because an agency cannot be all things to all people. Choices must be made and priorities must be set.

This is easier said than done, however. Not only is there a constant demand on social service agencies to meet society's overwhelming needs, but there are also many responses that appear to be appropriate. Because the pressures are ongoing and acute, the tendency is to try to "plug up the hole" or to "fill the vacuum."

This case study demonstrates how careful attention to and awareness of the mission of an agency can guide an organization's internal and external commitments. The theoretical model of agency development described here calls for ongoing consideration of an agency's fundamental purpose within the context of social change. Although the agency in this discussion, JEVS, had to deal with its uniqueness as a sectarian service, the fundamental problem of maintaining a commitment to the agency's mission remains the same for all social service agencies.

Chapter 6 examines the role of the administrator in shaping and protecting the agency's mission. It is the administrator's responsibility to protect the agency's identity and to suggest the appropriate strategies to retain its integrity.

6

The Administrator's Role in Agency Governance

In the search for an understanding of the functions of the administrator of a social service agency, it is essential to focus on the governance process. This chapter discusses policy making and the implications for administrative leadership, because "few functions are more demanding or vital for the administrator than the organization and maintenance of agency . . . boards through which agency policy is formulated" (Rosenthal & Young, 1980, p. 86). This discussion logically follows the preceding chapter because governance and policy making are inextricably intertwined with the agency's mission.

THE BOARD OF DIRECTORS

In recent years, largely as a result of the antipoverty programs of the 1960s, an interest in public policy and policy analysis has emerged; however, the policy-making function has a long history in the voluntary social service sector. The activities of concerned citizens who organize welfare services for various groups in need, both in sectarian and nonsectarian settings, is well documented and represents a delimited aspect of policy making. In fact, the involvement of laypeople on the policy level in social welfare antedates the existence of social work as a profession.

Although the boards of voluntary agencies originally comprised wealthy laypeople whose function was often to provide funds for the agency, with the advent of communitywide, federated fund raising, their functions have changed and broadened. Today, the board "represents the agency in community and inter-agency relationships, and most important, from the viewpoint of everyday welfare practice, it has the power to set policy in all phases of agency operation, from rules governing client eligibility to pay scales for professional staff" (Wilensky & Lebeaux, 1958, p. 269).

The role of the administrator vis-à-vis the board of directors is a complex one for several reasons. First, not only are administrators hired by the agency's board of directors, but the board also has the power to fire them; second, the board is usually composed of community elites, in contrast to the administrator, who is usually a member of the lower middle class and is upwardly mobile; third, the administrator is trained to protect professional social work values, knowledge, and skill, in contrast to the board members, whose expertise is usually in legal and fiscal matters.

In addressing these issues, Kramer (1969) suggests that this relationship works precisely because a balance is maintained. It is an exchange relationship whereby the administrator is supported by the board, while the board members get status and prestige from their agency role. Seeley (1957) documents the fact that board membership is often necessary for corporate advancement.

THE ROLE OF THE ADMINISTRATOR

The role of the administrator in interaction with the board of directors is multifaceted. Although the conventional understanding is that the board is responsible for determining policies and that the administrator is responsible for implementing those policies, in reality, the process is far from cut and dried. Most often, the administrator is critical in determining the nature and the extent of the relationship.

The most obvious and clear-cut roles of the administrator are in developing the budget and in hiring staff to carry out the policies through program implementation. It must be noted that in contrast to the administrator, who is involved with the agency on a full-time basis, the board members are volunteers who have primary responsibilities elsewhere. The administrator provides agency statistics, interprets client needs (present and future), discusses service options, and provides information on funding possibilities. When the board members are dependent in their decision making on the material supplied by the administrator, the administrator is very much part of the policy-making process.

The administrator can be proactive or reactive, content to rest on the agency's laurels, or innovative in responding to the rapidly changing needs in the community. The administrator of a family service agency, for example, can be content to support the stance that the agency continue business as usual with the traditional families in the community; alternatively, the administrator can seek to serve people who are part of the many new and unconventional family arrangements, including single heads of households, gay and lesbian partners with children, or families that have members with acquired immune deficiency syndrome. There is no question that the latter choice would be a more complicated, costly, and controversial route.

Another example of administrative choice is the decision concerning agency survival when the budget is not balanced. An administrator whose agency is experiencing financial hardship can opt to restrict service to paying clients and refer the poor population to a public agency. By contrast, the administrator who is a client advocate can call for the use of a portion of the agency's endowment funds, if such use is essential for the continuation of services for economically dependent clients.

One powerful tool that administrators have at their disposal is the ability to influence the composition of the board of directors to reflect the direction the administrator deems appropriate for agency growth and development. Board members can be selected for a variety of reasons, including their status in the community, their technical expertise (for example, lawyers and investment specialists), or their orientations toward community and client needs.

The theoretical model of social service agency development discussed in Chapter 4 provides a useful handle for dealing with the relationship between the administrator and the board of directors. An analysis of the organization's stage of development can help the administrator determine the appropriate role and composition of the board in relation to the agency's direction and desired direction for change.

For example, a community-organized medical clinic in its first stage of development would be concerned with meeting the basic primary-care needs of its community on a quantitative basis and would not want to leave the decisions regarding the nature and distribution of services to physicians. The board of directors at this stage would require members from the community who are informed about the health care needs and priorities of the local population. Once the basic needs for general medical care were met and the service structure was established, the needs for higher quality, specialized care would, appropriately, require greater professional authority. The board of directors would then benefit from members who had more specialized medical expertise.

POLICY ISSUES OF ADMINISTRATIVE CONCERN

It is helpful to understand some of the critical issues and dilemmas that are addressed in the governance process of social service agencies. Gurin (1978) cogently highlights several of these that are of long-standing and central concern.

One of the earliest dilemmas experienced by the social work profession stems from its historical origins. The social work profession evolved from two distinct directions: The first was that of the friendly visitor who worked with individuals in need; the second was the settlement house worker who was community based and reform oriented.

Morris and Anderson (1975) call attention to the fact that this dichotomy is a critical issue even today. The language may vary but the message is the same. Although Lee (1937) used the terms "cause" versus "function" to describe the dichotomy, Morris and Anderson use the terms "care" versus "cure." Thus, the friendly visitors of the Charity Organization were direct service oriented and focused on client care and agency function. This is in contrast to the settlement house workers, who were interested in social causes and societal cures.

This issue is at the heart of the policy and management process in social agencies because choices must be made. Can an agency do both, or must a clear priority be set?

This issue is not an academic one. The distinction was at the heart of the dilemma faced in the early years of the community mental health centers (CMHCs). A radically new structure for the care of those with mental health problems and mentally retarded individuals was designed at the federal level by the Mental Retardation and Community Mental Health Construction Act of 1963.

Two basic changes illustrate the care versus cure dilemma. First, there was a shift from the traditional one-to-one relationship between the psychiatrist and the patient, with its emphasis on the individual's adjustment to a community-oriented, broad-spectrum approach. Second, a public health focus on the prevention of illness and the promotion of health was added to the medically based, treatment-oriented system.

The notion of prevention in the field of mental health was a new and precarious one (Perlmutter & Silverman, 1973). The process was complicated because the CMHC's mission was not defined by that agency's board of directors; rather, the mandate was externally developed by federal legislation. Because the local board was not involved in setting agency policy, but functioned only in an advisory capacity, the administrator had to play a critical role in the protection and implementation of CMHC policies.

The abdication of leadership was demonstrated in a study that found that the administrators did not differ from other professionals in the organization with regard to the new goal of prevention (Perlmutter & Vayda, 1978). CMHC administrators could have played a proactive leadership role by educating the centers' boards of directors regarding the benefits that would result from the legislation. Instead, they remained committed to the traditional treatment technology and ideology.

In addition to the issue of care versus cure, how should social work deal with the issues of effectiveness versus efficiency? In the early years of voluntary social service agency activity, effectiveness was the central criterion for service, and services were ipso facto accepted at face value. With the advent of the public programs of the 1970s, the notions of program evaluation, accountability, and efficiency were introduced (Newman & Turem, 1974).

A recently emerging issue of central concern at the social policy level is that of privatization. Increasingly, in contrast to traditional nonprofit agencies, there are profit-making agencies in the social service sector. Social service agencies are also being pressured to consider alternative means of raising funds, because public funds have become less available for social service, and community funds, through United Way, have not kept pace with society's needs. Consequently, in addition to seeking funds from foundations, some agencies have become, or are about to become, involved in profit-making ventures (Perlmutter & Adams, 1990).

Finally, it is important that an additional policy issue be identified: the structure of governance. Interest in this area relates to citizen and consumer participation and to self-help or participatory management, which are explained in greater detail in the next section.

These policy issues, among others, are illustrative of the matters that require administrative consideration, analysis, and decision making. How they are handled is a clear reflection of leadership style. Gurin (1978) focuses on the relationship between policy analysis and management, suggesting that "policy is never settled for all time but involves a continuous process of negotiation in which management is necessarily engaged" (p. 296).

THE STRUCTURE OF GOVERNANCE

Citizen or consumer participation and participatory management present important opportunities and alternatives in the structure of governance. Both merit serious consideration on the part of the administrator, especially because the profession's value system supports these structures.

Citizen participation and self-management are related subjects, because both deal with the empowerment of new constituencies: consumers and workers. Citizen participation, a legacy of the 1960s, is discussed here first. In the 1960s, for the first time, the participation of consumers in affecting the policies of the agencies from which they received services was given credence over the traditional participation of the social elites who were not consumers of the agency's services. This notion has become a fact of social service agency life, although it is imperfectly implemented.

An interesting cross-national example of citizen participation is in Yugoslavia where the political ideology emphasized the involvement of the citizenry at all levels, from the smallest local work unit to the national level of government (Perlmutter, 1974). The importance of that ideology, which is relevant to the concerns described here, is that the citizenry was considered "less and less the subject and more and more the creator and implementor of the social policy" (Vajs, 1973, p. 5).

Participatory management also began to receive serious attention in the 1960s (Gruber, 1983) when appropriate new structures for the governance of social service agencies were sought. Experimentation in different models of decision making began to take place in the human services, usually in small agencies in the voluntary sector. Although large public bureaucracies are less receptive to these changes, new innovations have been taking place there as well. Weil (1988), for example, describes an alternative program in the Los Angeles County Department of Children's Services that developed a partnership with self-help client groups.

Clearly, these new patterns reflect broad societal shifts. The administrator either can continue to work in a traditional mode or can seek to become informed about the pros and cons and the costs and benefits of new governance mechanisms to provide leadership in the agency as it seeks to define its appropriate governance structure.

CREATIVE APPROACHES TO GOVERNANCE

Several case examples highlight some unconventional approaches to governance. The illustrations are from three alternative funds, which have been developed to offer donors options for making contributions to social service agencies other than through the United Way (Perlmutter, 1989).

Although these organizations are atypical of traditional social service agencies in that they offer alternative services and governance arrangements, they are of heuristic value for five reasons: (1) they effectively use specific criteria for board membership, (2) they link organizational mission and stage of development with board selection, (3) they focus on both care and cure, (4) they give priority to both consumer participation and participatory management, and (5) they promote an active relationship between policy and management.

Women's Way is a fund composed of nine member agencies that view as their goals the empowerment of women and the changing attitudes, laws, and institutions that perpetuate the problems faced by women. Women's Way is clear in its intent to give member agencies an active role in policy making, compatible with its philosophy of empowerment. Although the governing board consists of representatives from both member agencies and the community at large, care has been taken to ensure that the agencies have the majority of seats. Consequently, there are two representatives from each member agency of Women's Way and a nearly equal number of at-large representatives. The criteria for member agencies are clearly delineated vis-à-vis the ideology and mission of Women's Way, ensuring that policy will be set within the given framework.

Another example of creative approaches to governance is that of the Bread and Roses Community Fund. Guided by the motto "change, not charity," this group targets its funding to local advocacy organizations, with priority given to community-based organizations that have limited access to traditional funding sources because they are considered too small, too new, or too controversial. It is a membership organization composed of donors, volunteers, and grantee organization representatives and is unusual in that all its members meet annually to elect two boards. The board of directors is responsible for all policy and procedural decisions except those dealing with funding. The Community Funding Board deals with all aspects of funding, including applications, allocations, grant-making policies, and procedural decisions.

Guidelines have been developed for both Bread and Roses boards to ensure representation by people of color, women, and sexual minorities; donors and grantees must also be represented. One staff member also serves on each board. To ensure communication and cooperation between the boards, there are two seats from the Community Funding Board on the board of directors. Furthermore, the majority of members on the funding board must be community activists.

In contrast to the boards of directors of traditional social service agencies, Bread and Roses seeks to ensure a broad donor pool; any person who contributes $50 or more can serve on the board. This is a critical stipulation because more than 50 percent of the donors are wealthy. By this rule, the fund ensures a balanced board without undue influence by a small cadre of its wealthy donors.

The Black United Fund is another alternative fund that illustrates innovative governance. It seeks to "support projects that have a positive and continuous impact on the lives of black people in health and human services, education, criminal justice, arts and culture, economic development, leadership development, and emergency needs" (Black United Fund of Pennsylvania, 1986, p. 1). Its board of directors, which sets policy, is composed of members who are recruited from a broad array of local organizations and who must be at least 18 years old. Members are recruited from the clergy and from the legal, social work, accounting, and business professions. In addition, the Black United Fund has an advisory board that is made up of community members who work on special projects (that is, fund raising) and who act as liaisons with labor organizations, churches, and the community. The board of directors is also actively involved in program development for the fund.

All three of these alternative funds have a mechanism that ensures the rotation of board members. Although the terms and mechanisms vary according to the particular needs of the programs, all are concerned with the representation of points of view that reflect commitment to the funds' missions.

The leaders of these organizations have served a critical role in the development of their governance mechanisms. All the agencies have female executive directors who give extensively of their time and energy. The salaries of the administrators are not commensurate with their competence or function. It is clear that they are directly contributing to the survival of each of these funds.

A FINAL WORD ON AGENCY GOVERNANCE

Boards of directors carry the legal responsibility and sanction for the agencies that they govern. It is clear, however, that their roles are dramatically shaped by and dependent on the administrators of their agencies.

The aim of this discussion has been to acquaint the reader with some of the issues that administrators must deal with as part of their normal workload. It is fair to state that the work the administrator performs with the board of directors is one of the more critical aspects of the job and requires careful and creative leadership.

7

The Administrator as Politician

In most organizations that provide professional services, such as medicine, engineering, or social work, the route to the executive suite is charted by one's movement up the professional rungs. The implicit assumption is that if one is good at laying on hands, that is, providing a technical service, one can be effective at helping others lay on hands, and the movement is up the hierarchy of an organization. Yet, clinical skills do not ipso facto translate into administrative skills, even for first-class professionals. This is not to say that the concern is with the Peter principle, whereby less than competent people are moved up to get them out. The concern is with qualified, competent, and meritorious practitioners.

Chapter 3 discussed Levinson and Klerman's (1967) thesis that the shift to administration is similar to a major life-cycle developmental change and that a personal transformation is called for to achieve a new professional identity. Levinson and Klerman's (1972) subsequent emphasis on the management of external boundaries was also noted. It is this continuing need to explore the administrator's role regarding power, politics, and external boundaries that guides this discussion of other central administrative functions. The particular interest here is in the practical consequences for the practicing administrator, because professionalism and politics are not disparate or incongruent activities. Rather, the social work administrator is the link between professionalism and politics.

Gummer (1990), an astute commentator on the politics of social work administration, addresses the various political processes inherent in social welfare organizations. He attends to the internal organizational politics with a focus on micro- and macro-level interests in his discussion of the politics of money, people, program implementation, and ethics; he also highlights the social service agency's environment outside of the organizational boundaries.

The social work administrator must be effective both internally and externally. As the external environment is becoming simultaneously more complex, dense, and unpredictable, special attention must be paid to new skills and strategies appropriate for a new political reality.

Gummer (1984) aptly describes the complexity of social work administration as follows:

> The reader [might be left] with the impression that politics is all there is to administrative work. This was not my intention. Administrators must attend to several other concerns beside the political. There are the pragmatic realities of the daily operations of complex organizations and programs; the technical challenges of adapting advances in management science to the operational needs of social agencies; and the professional concerns of designing programs that are informed by what is known about the best ways of providing help to people. Politics has been singled out both because of its critical role in social agency administration and its growing importance in administrative practices. (pp. 33–34)

Gummer's work is important because it helps to shape a political paradigm for analyzing the work of the social work administrator. The next section of this chapter discusses the current political environment as the context for the discussion of the administrator's role.

THE POLITICAL CONTEXT OF ADMINISTRATIVE PRACTICE: OLD WINE IN NEW BOTTLES

The effects of the presidential elections of the 1980s continue to reverberate throughout American society as social programs are curtailed, dismembered, and dropped. The philosophical underpinnings that shape the social work profession have been called into question. This is indeed a shift for many social workers who were reared in a society that supported federal leadership in social programs, that provided services to a variety of populations in need, and that encouraged labor development in human service. It is unnecessary to describe all the changes in detail, but it is important to highlight the changes in ideology and national commitment.

In a provocative paper, Stern (1984) suggests that the current national mood is not a detour from the American social welfare tradition. He argues that the conditions that made possible the New Deal of the 1930s and the Poverty Program of the 1960s are no longer functional and that, consequently, this society is in for a long siege in this new social environment. The split between the poor and the nonpoor, between the blue-collar ethnics and African Americans, has long-term consequences. He suggests that social administrators must develop "a new set of skills designed to maximize agency goals and to minimize the adverse effect on client populations" (p. 19). He describes the effects of reactive strategies that allow Americans to win some battles and lose the war. He calls, instead, for "imaginative program and policy development and an increased effort to understand and correct the crippling divisions in American society, often based on class and race" (p. 19).

Stern's analysis stimulates an examination of a long-range view of the politics of social work administration. The more immediate realities faced by the administrator in dealing with policy and politics are discussed below.

POLICY AND POLITICS

Because the areas of policy and politics are so closely intertwined, it is essential for the social work administrator to be clear about their similarities and differences. Policy is defined as program intentions that reflect decisions made on the basis of principles with supporting rationales; politics is viewed as the actions of interest groups who are trying to affect or are affected by policies. The administrator must be well versed in both policy and politics.

Four policy constraints can be identified: sophisticated managerial responses are required to deal with mandates that are competing, conflicting, ambiguous, or incompatible (Perlmutter, 1980). Each constraint stems from external sources but is inextricably linked to internal operations.

Competing mandates result when several policies that underpin a program are appropriate both on their own terms and with each other. A problem arises when no clear priorities have been set and resources are inadequate to support both programs. For example, the Mental Retardation and Community Mental Health Construction Act of 1963 mandated prevention and treatment as part of the program's mission. As a result, from its inception, there were strains in community mental health centers that reflected not only ideological and professional problems but also administrative problems (Perlmutter, 1973 a,b; Perlmutter & Silverman, 1972; Perlmutter & Vayda, 1978).

In dealing with competing mandates, the appropriate strategy may be to garner increased resources to be able to fulfill the competing mandates simultaneously. If increased resources cannot be obtained, ordering of priorities and long-range planning are necessary to ensure that both mandates are met.

In the case of conflicting mandates, the administrator usually must choose to support one or the other mandate, not both. It is necessary to examine the options and choose the one that is most appropriate to the agency's developmental stage. In some cases, an innovative administrator can use his or her analytical skills to redefine the problem and find different alternatives based on a new perspective.

Ambiguous mandates, which occur when expectations are unclear, can be used as an opportunity for creative leadership. The administrator who is a risk-taker can take advantage of the lack of clarity and press for unconventional options and new directions. A less imaginative administrator might press for clarification of the policies and thus lose an opportunity for innovation. Furthermore, in the press for greater clarity, the administrator could precipitate a less satisfactory situation, particularly if an ambiguous mandate is reformulated into a competing or conflicting one.

Incompatible mandates reflect the different expectations of federal, state, and local governments and create another administrative bind. Because public policy drives not only public but also voluntary agencies to an increasing degree, the expectations from each level of government are often diverse, and access to each level requires different skills (that is discussed in greater detail in the next section of this chapter). Policy is clearly bound to politics, and the administrator must become adept at differentiating the political skills needed to work effectively not only with bureaucracies at different levels, but also with the broad array of interest groups at several levels.

ADMINISTRATIVE STRATEGIES

There is currently much discussion in the professional literature concerning administrative strategies for survival. Here the focus is on three approaches for proactive leadership linked to the preceding discussion of policies and politics: (1) working with the state system, (2) redesigning the voluntary sector, and (3) pursuing legal options. Each of these strategies is directed toward the external boundaries of the human service system, as suggested by Levinson and Klerman (1972). In addition, each of the strategies requires political sophistication, as called for by Gummer (1984).

Working with the State System

The role of the federal government in social service has received a great deal of attention. An article by Radin (1983) examines the differences between the federal government's role in the 1960s and its role in the 1980s and notes that the roles of the state and local public sectors, as well as the private sector, are increasing as federal involvement is curtailed. Given this reality, it is urgent that serious attention be paid to state government and its role in the provision of human services. Bevilacqua (1984) fears that the current interest in state government may be superficial, a fad, because too often the perception of state government focuses on patronage, inefficiency, and bureaucratism. Lynn (1980) discusses the states' interest in economy and efficiency and the problem that "professional human service agencies, and their associated interest groups, in general, do not have the same standing with governors, legislators and county commissioners as they do in Congress" (p. 18).

Bevilacqua carefully dissects the operations of the state system to explore the critical issues as well as to expose those areas of operation that could be accessible to human service administrators. Before one can develop strategies, however, it is necessary to understand the system. Bevilacqua (1984) pays attention to the duality of professional values as opposed to political ideology. The social work administrator must recognize and deal with the dilemmas involved in managing conflicting demands. For example:

> Double standards of care, professional credentials, financing mechanisms and professional education are illustrative of the more obvious ones. It is at the state level of government where many of these issues are most visible and where their solutions rest within the political process. The policies that are developed, changed and redesigned challenge a set of values that are diverse and often contradictory. Successful government managers must recognize and understand this process. (p. 82)

As a politician, the social work administrator must be aware of the political ideology that informs the behavior of governors and legislators at the state level, where pragmatism overrides ideology. Thus, managers of state agencies "are very cautious in promoting any specific point of view. A kind of homogenization takes place. . . . Dealing directly with ideology is usually avoided" (Bevilacqua, 1984, p. 83). This is bound to create internal conflict.

An understanding of this reality is essential for the administrator to begin to develop effective approaches. Bevilacqua calls for a blending of political with professional skills. He notes that when candidates for state positions are screened, the emphasis is on professional credentials and little is asked concerning their ability to articulate policy or to communicate effectively with the public. It is therefore not surprising, given the realities of the job, that the average tenure for mental health commissioners, for example, is only 18 months.

Dissection of the anatomy of the state system provides clues to access. First, the governor's office, the executive branch, must be understood as an important point of entry, including the realities of succession and the statutory limitations on terms of office. This also means that the administrator should get to know members of the governor's immediate staff and their relationships to the established agencies and their heads. An understanding of the budget office, which is within the executive branch, is equally critical, because there is an inherent tension between program and budget staffs.

Second, it is essential to examine the linkages among the three branches of government, as well as to have access to key legislators and committees. Third, although commissioners are political appointees, management in the bureaucracy is ongoing; it is important to develop linkages at both the upper- and middle-management levels. Finally, the organization and mobilization of constituencies are essential and include consumers, providers, advocates, and professional associations. Constituencies link political, professional, and consumer interests. Not only are the political skills important, but also the basic skill of community organizing is a sine qua non.

Redesigning the Voluntary Sector

The voluntary sector, the traditional backbone of social work programs, is being revitalized in response to the shift in and diminution of public responsibility. It is time to reexamine the structure of this system, because it was originally designed and developed in a very different historical context.

The following strategies are selected as illustrative of the leadership activity needed to ensure the viability and effectiveness of the voluntary sector. Social work administrators must help their voluntary agencies to engage in strategic planning as they examine their raison d'être, including the system variables of mission, services, and target populations discussed in Chapter 4. Business as usual, or organizational maintenance, cannot be continued when the external environment is so dramatically shifting. The planning must encompass not only the internal capacity, but also the external capacity in the broader community as well.

Consequently, administrators, as well as their agencies, must become politically sophisticated and sharpen their skills in this arena. Administrators, for example, are in a unique position to know the consequences of the deregulation of many social programs. Although advocacy has always been viewed as a vital part of the social work profession's armamentarium, it must now be fine-tuned, expanded, and developed.

> Advocacy in the halls of government can represent another form of agency response . . . even by those voluntary agencies which . . . will opt to forego further governmental funding. . . .
>
> The political agenda of social agencies should include the advocacy of expanding incentives for charitable contributions and strong opposition to any effort to restrict non-partisan, issue-oriented advocacy by nonprofit organizations. These are recurring concerns which should be on the long-range political agenda for social agencies.
>
> The same holds true for the development of coalitions beyond the social agency network under whatever auspices. . . . Citizen organizations concerned with consumer issues, the environment, and the urban condition represent logical allies. Neither the business community nor the labor movement should be assumed by definition to be protagonists or antagonists. (Kahn, 1984, p. 66)

It is essential to remember that coalitions coalesce around single issues, and Kahn (1984) points out that "political pragmatism is not synonymous with unethical behavior" (p. 67). This reinforces the notion of the administrator as politician.

Pursuing Legal Options

The final external political strategy to be discussed here concerns the pursuit of legal remedies. This is an area that is usually unfamiliar to social work administrators, who often view it as being beyond their ken. Yet, it is a powerful mechanism that merits attention in these critical times (Herr, Arons, & Wallace, 1983). Again, a case study is used to illustrate this concept (Weiner, 1984).

The Department of Public Welfare (DPW), a state agency, placed severe limitations on the reimbursements for methadone maintenance and psychotherapy services to patients needing medical assistance. The medical implications were grave because the curtailment threatened the viability of the entire statewide methadone program, which was being delivered by nonprofit vendors. The response of the various methadone program administrators was immediately to begin coalition building among all the program directors in a large urban area. The response was varied, each reflecting the vulnerability of their respective programs. For example, those who were least threatened were most cautious in their response.

At first, the administrators identified an array of options ranging from the least to the most militant, as follows: write letters to DPW, meet with DPW officials in an attempt to negotiate a compromise, meet with state legislators, enlist the support of community leaders, use the news media to publicize the issue, and initiate a lawsuit.

Each of the first five strategies was attempted by the providers, but it became evident that the strategy used by DPW was to divide and conquer as it informed state legislators that the problem was unique to the one urban area and had little relevance on a statewide basis. This pushed the administrators to exercise the sixth political strategy, that of going to court. They won.

Weiner (1984) pays attention to the risks involved in political strategies and addresses the political skills that are necessary. He suggests not only that several strategies must be pursued simultaneously, but also that the administrator must be ready "to switch quickly as opportunities present themselves" (p. 210). A sense of timing is important, as is the need for creativity. The issues must have an "emotional as well as an intellectual impact" to enlist the support of broader constituencies (p. 210). Finally, a critical element in the art of political effectiveness is the recognition that it is essential that the most powerful interest group with a stake in the problem carry the ball. In this case The Hospital Association, a statewide organization with direct involvement because of the many hospital-based methadone programs, prepared the lawsuit against DPW and won.

A FINAL WORD ON ADMINISTRATION AND POLITICS

This chapter focused on the role of the administrator as politician. It identified several areas for action, all external to the social service agency, and presented a case illustration of the political activity on the part of social work administrators.

It is clear that the social work administrator is involved in politics in all aspects of the social service agency. The creative and sensitive use of the political process therefore becomes a central challenge.

8

The Administrator and Interorganizational Relations

This chapter examines those professional relationships that must be nurtured across the external boundaries of an agency. Although the external environment always requires political sophistication, as discussed in Chapter 7, the topics to be discussed here have a different thrust. More directly related to the services that the agency provides, these include information and referral arrangements, case management and service coordination, community-based strategic planning, and public relations and development.

It is helpful to recognize that an exchange relationship exists whenever several agencies or organizations are involved in collaborative activity (Levine & White, 1961). There must be a quid pro quo for all parties concerned, because organizations do not operate out of altruistic motivation. Each of the topics discussed here is best understood by keeping this underlying assumption in mind, and it is certainly essential that the administrator be aware of this reality to maximize the agency's return in the exchange.

The elements implicit in these relationships are presented and illustrated with case material. It should be noted that interorganizational relations are very fluid, often reflecting the social policy fads of the day. Consequently, the administrator must be careful in examining the interorganizational alternatives and making the appropriate choices.

INFORMATION AND REFERRAL

Just as hospitals are dependent on their patient count, so, too, are social agencies dependent on their client census. Often, the availability of clients is linked to several factors that are independent of the initiatives of the administrator. In the extreme case in which there is only one agency providing the service, for example, the clients will be captive. Even in more usual circumstances, however, there is certainly much room for administrative leadership to ensure that the essential functions of information and referral are operating at their maximum effectiveness. Several studies from both the voluntary and the public social service sectors serve to illustrate the problems and potentials in this arena.

The role of the administrator in developing the information and referral aspect of the system is linked to the organization's stage of development, as discussed in Chapter 4. In the voluntary sector, for example, The Jewish Employment and Vocational Service (JEVS), the subject of the case study presented in Chapter 5, effectively demonstrates the relationship between the agency's stage and the information and referral activity.

In stage 1, self-interest, a priority is placed on serving as many clients as possible to meet the social problem that led to the founding of the agency. The emphasis is on the quantity, as opposed to the quality, of the service that is provided. The rush to serve occurred in JEVS to the extent that even the members of the board of directors were involved in the provision of services. Because the agency was organized to meet the needs of the Jewish community stemming both from the influx of Jewish people to the United States after World War II and from indigenous anti-Semitism in the United States, JEVS decided that only Jewish clients would be served. All outreach to other agencies, for both information and referral, remained within the Jewish community. Thus, major external relationships were with Jewish agencies locally and with the national coordinating agency for all Jewish vocational services, the Jewish Occupational Council.

After World War II, however, the external environment shifted, requiring new policy decisions linked to the agency's mission:

> The matter of accepting non-Jewish war veterans was brought up for discussion. After a great deal of discussion it was agreed that non-Jewish war veterans should not be turned away; also some handicapped cases might be accepted. This procedure will be tried as an experiment to see whether or not it will tax the facilities of the agency too much. (JEVS, 1945)

This was a critical decision in terms of the agency's development. It paved the way for a broader definition of agency clients and services that was linked to the shift to stage 2, professionalism. Non-Jewish clients were served increasingly, but were served through programs developed with government funds. The services became more sophisticated, reflecting newly emerging professional trends.

There was then a dramatic shift in intersystem relationships. Not only was there an active engagement with public sector funds and programs for information and referral services, but, in addition, the agency became actively involved with nonsectarian agencies in the broader local community (for example, the Health and Welfare Council). The self-conscious outreach to other agencies appropriate to JEVS's stage of development became an important administrative strategy.

As for information and referral in the public sector in general, public welfare agencies are increasingly dependent on outside social service systems in both the nonprofit and profit-making sectors to provide social service to their clients through the purchase of services or other contracts. The availability of these services to public assistance clients is problematic, however, because agencies are "wary of sharing in the stigma attached to heavy involvement with the economically dependent portion of the population" (Kronick et al., 1973, p. 52). It is therefore crucial that public agencies concentrate on outreach to these outside agencies to increase the availability of their services to economically dependent clients.

For example, given that the intent of the community mental health center (CMHC) legislation in 1963 was to serve all citizens regardless of their income level, the question of interest is whether public welfare agencies used this service potential. A study was conducted to examine the level of awareness and utilization of CMHCs by social service staffs in two public agencies (Perlmutter, Yudin, & Heinemann, 1974): a county board of assistance, which provided financial supports, and a family service division of a department of public welfare, which provided social service. Although awareness of and referrals to CMHCs were significantly higher in the social service agency than they were in the public assistance agency, utilization was low in comparison with that of other gatekeeper groups, such as school counselors.

This was a serious omission on the part of the public agencies because there are so few resources available to these populations. Although the truth of the matter may be that CMHCs' outreach efforts were not directed toward the public welfare system, it was all the more the responsibility of the welfare administrator to seek out actively and aggressively those services that were intended to serve all citizens in the catchment area.

This study leads to a generalization regarding agency leadership. The approach must be two-pronged. First, administrators must be active in initiating interorganizational negotiations with an array of agencies that offer services appropriate for their clientele. Second, the administrator must be certain that the agency staff is informed about these resources and trained in the art of referral through staff development programs and supervision. The latter point is an important one, in light of the findings of the study; different approaches to making referrals were evident. Seventy-seven percent of the family workers who made referrals had telephoned CMHC for their clients, whereas only 23 percent of the income maintenance staff had done so; 30 percent of the family workers had personally escorted their clients to CMHC, whereas no county board of assistance worker had done this. The active involvement of the worker in making the referral unquestionably increases the probability that the client will be served by a new agency.

This point is corroborated when one examines the experience of CMHC in regard to its information and referral sources (Perlmutter et al., 1974). An intensive effort to publicize CMHC in one catchment area resulted in the raising of awareness of three gatekeeper groups and an increase in their utilization of the center. It should be noted that not only was utilization increased, but the level of satisfaction with the services used was higher as well. Furthermore, among the three gatekeeper groups studied (that is, doctors, school counselors, and members of the clergy), the response was greatest among the school counselors, for whom a work-related and systematic orientation was part of the working situation. This suggests that special attention should be paid to linkages with those points in the doctor's and clergy's professional development at which systematic contact is possible—in medical and divinity graduate programs as well as through professional societies.

The main point is that it is an administrative responsibility to foster information and referral services through formal interorganizational negotiations. It cannot be assumed that frontline workers will automatically be externally oriented, a major finding of a demonstration project whose major thrust was an external, community-oriented one (Kronick et al., 1973).

This demonstration was designed to test a new service delivery model designed by the American Public Welfare Association. Its major intent was to expand social service through the mobilization of existing services on behalf of the client and the expansion of existing resources and the creation of new ones through community organization and outreach. The findings showed a highly internally oriented agency that placed emphasis on the effective functioning of its internal components. Evidently, the activities provided for in the

American Public Welfare Association model were inadequately developed in practice. This can be explained in large part by the lack of forceful administrative direction and support in developing contractual relationships with other agencies.

All of these examples attest to the importance of appropriate interorganizational relationships in increasing the effectiveness of information and referral activities. All three cases also demonstrate the centrality of administrative leadership in this domain.

CASE MANAGEMENT AND SERVICES COORDINATION

Case management has been as elusive a goal in public welfare as Moby Dick was to Captain Ahab. The quest continues with the hope that the human service system will be more successful in achieving its objective than was Captain Ahab in his. To succeed, however, administrators must be realistic about the context within which they operate and not just idealistic about the outcomes they wish to attain.

In the early 1970s a concern about service delivery systems was manifested at the federal level; services were viewed as uncoordinated, fragmented, rigid, and unresponsive. To remedy the situation, objectives were articulated that proposed to coordinate delivery, provide comprehensive local services, and plan for rational local resource allocation (Gage, 1976). Federal legislation, which was passed with the objective of promoting coordination of services, included Title 3 of the Older Americans Act that was passed in 1973 and Title XX of the 1974 Social Service Amendments, among others. In that same period, social service critics such as Rosenberg and Brody (1974) identified the problem of service fragmentation as being reflective of specific agency mandates.

The federal legislation made possible some important demonstration projects at the state and local levels, with many important lessons to be learned from these projects related to case management. Steinberg and Carter (1983) expanded the discussion from a focus on the level of the social service manager to the level of the administrator. Their discussion was based on a rational model that suggested that if one could clearly identify the service pathway of the necessary administrative roles, the problems could be handled and the services could be coordinated.

Regardless of the clarity of the administrative leadership or the coherence of the case management pathway, the external context of public policy creates internal contradictions, a catch-22 bind. This discussion of case management, accordingly, focuses on both the external political context and the administrative role.

The external political context must be understood in any attempt to develop a case management system. Because social service agencies usually seek to protect their particular domains, an external impetus for change is necessary to set the system in motion. This external clout can be varied in nature. For example, in the American Public Welfare Association project discussed previously, the impetus was a demonstration grant; in the United Services Agency project in Wilkes-Barre, Pennsylvania, it was the devastating flood of 1972 and the political efforts of U.S. Congressman James Flood that served as the critical impetus (Perlmutter, Richan, & Weirich, 1977).

Another critical element is the charismatic leadership available to initiate case management efforts. In the case of the United Services Agency, it was the regional secretary of the Pennsylvania Department of Public Welfare who was the charismatic figure. She was respected not only at the state level, but also in both the public and voluntary sectors at the local level. Although charismatic leadership is necessary to induce changes in systems, it is in itself insufficient. The leader must be politically astute and able to muster a strong local base of support for follow-up and stabilization. If this is not attended to, the initial impetus can fail, because charismatic leadership is most effective at the start-up phase of any program.

Another critical element in the larger system is the policy base that underpins the case management effort. The critical question is, where does the sanction for the effort lie in the long run? A major problem with case management and services coordination is that all too often each participating program stems from a separate policy base that may, in fact, be incompatible with the coordinating effort.

The role of central administration, as discussed previously, is central to the effective implementation of any case management program. First and foremost, there must be clarity at the top regarding not only the plan but also the implementation necessary to achieve the objective. In addition, there is an unusual and more extensive array of elements that must be orchestrated than there is in a single agency jurisdiction, to use Slavin's (1980) metaphor of the administrator as conductor. Responsible leadership must understand that the administrative role varies with the different needs of the case management system as it develops.

Although administrative clarity is necessary, it is insufficient. Consistency throughout the system is another essential element. In the United Services Agency project, the various actors included the Pennsylvania Department of Public Welfare, the county commissioners, and the county agencies, as well as the human service agencies in the voluntary sector. Unfortunately, there was a lack of consistent interest and support not only among people at the different levels, but also among the actors involved at the same level.

Thus, for example, when special fiscal arrangements were necessary to accomplish the case management objectives, the state budget office was inflexible and expected business as usual from the individual participating programs (that is, mental health, aging, and child welfare). In addition, although five service centers were organized in five communities to allow for easy access in the widespread county area, each local center ran its shop autonomously with different patterns of service. Central administration did not have enough strength to implement uniform service arrangements compatible with the project's case management objectives.

Advisory committees can be helpful in the design and development of any case management effort because they can provide legitimacy to the effort. They require a great investment of administrative time, however, in their selection and structuring. In addition, members must be trained and educated in regard to the ongoing requirements of the case management program.

It is also essential to examine the cultures of the different participating organizations. There will be similarities and differences in regard to values, constraints, and turf. To ignore these differences is to court disaster.

Administrators bear the responsibility for interpreting the objectives and explaining the program to all participating staff members, especially because of the interdependence of all elements in this complex effort. Specifically, how does a particular social worker's role link to the achievement of the case management objectives that ultimately deal with meeting consumer needs?

Finally, attention must be paid to the use of incentives, recognition, and rewards. Staff members working at the front line experience great tension and frustration, which often culminate in burnout. Frontline staff members often pay the price for the inconsistencies that take place elsewhere in the system, be it at the policy level, the administrative level, or the client level. An area worthy of special administrative attention is how to help social workers enjoy and be stimulated by the challenges of case management (Weil, Karls, & Associates, 1985).

STRATEGIC PLANNING

Kahn (1984) suggests that strategic planning in the voluntary sector is essential for ensuring its viability and effectiveness. Business as usual and organizational maintenance must give way to a critical examination not only of individual agencies but also of the system of agencies involved in meeting communal needs.

> The current existence of an institution with all of its subunits is not in itself justification for continuation. In most instances, services being delivered, client needs, effectiveness of programs, and similar factors justify continuity. The changes in governmental funding streams and policies . . . create the need for many agencies to consider their future directions. . . . Parenthetically, a decision not to continue with current services need not mean the automatic termination of an agency. . . . Emphasis on service delivery needs to be the bedrock of the social agency's strategic planning. (p. 61)

Agencies must be ready to examine an array of service modalities, including mergers, conglomerates, and relationships between for-profit and not-for-profit organizations, among others. Kahn argues that "the levels of inter-organizational collaboration developed over the years appear to be far less than what is feasible and warranted under current circumstances" (p. 63).

Although cost-sharing and mergers are increasingly used in other sectors of society, including business and public education, they have not been evident in the human services. The Greater New York Fund/United Way (1981) addresses this matter in a volume entitled *Merger: Another Path Ahead*. The discussion explores the definitions, rationales, procedures, critical issues, and consequences of mergers and provides case examples to help clarify the process. The report emphasizes that although each merger is unique, there are common principles and processes that can help inform the administrative decision as to how to proceed. "Merger can be a path ahead, and those pioneers who set out on the path with foreknowledge of possibilities and pitfalls, are likely to be best equipped for the journey" (p. 17).

PUBLIC RELATIONS AND DEVELOPMENT

Social work, as well as the other human service professions, has been internally oriented, with little attention paid to the problem of communicating its special concerns and competencies to the broader society. This discussion includes the area of development in the section on public relations because both activities are clearly directed at tertiary constituencies outside of the immediate agency purview.

In an important volume, *Mass Media and Human Services*, Brawley (1983) discusses the urgency for reaching the public, identifies some of the priorities to be set in this effort, and provides important technical advice on how to do it. There has been relatively little concern about public relations, a subject that merits considerable attention (Goldman, 1960; President's Commission on Mental Health, 1978).

Brawley (1983) examines specific areas of consumer need, such as prevention of mental illness and self-help, and suggests that the mass media provides an excellent channel for promulgating these efforts. The various media forms offer unequaled possibilities, and it is important to understand the special access routes to effective use of newspapers, magazines, radio, and television. Thus, for example, even the difference between UHF (ultra high frequency) and VHF (very high frequency) is discussed in relation to selecting appropriate strategies (pp. 195–197).

Development, similarly, is a long-neglected area for administrative attention. It has become a highly visible and important part of the business and political worlds, but it is only beginning to be addressed in the human services sector. Cooper (1983) discusses market strategies for hospitals and suggests that they will need to apply such business concepts as "market share, product quality, R and D [research and development] expenditures, investment intensity, productivity and diversification" (p. 15). Because human service organizations are even more investment intensive than many profit-making companies are, their expenditures must be carefully made and must be clearly linked to the agency's objectives.

The administrator bears primary responsibility for development. In a small agency, the administrator may actually have to do the work, whereas in larger settings there may be a part-time development officer who must work closely with the administrator and have his or her full trust. The development officer develops a list of foundations whose interests are compatible with those of the agency and submits the proposal to the board of directors with the administrator's approval. The administrator serves as the link to the board of directors to keep it intimately involved with this function.

The administrator must understand the function of development and provide an appropriate structure wherein the activity is lodged. In addition to work with the board of directors, the professional staff must also be involved. Staff members should be encouraged to write proposals, perhaps through incentives such as salary increases and funds for travel. Staff initiatives and creative ideas must be supported and encouraged through an environment that is oriented to development.

The potential return for the agency of a well-designed development program cannot be overestimated, and the administrator is the one who must set it in motion. It is often tempting to "go for broke," to try everything and anything in the quest for resources. Again, the model of social agency development can serve to set the boundaries for what is desirable. It is important that the administrator provide leadership that protects the integrity and the direction of the organization so that the mandates of the agency drive the development directions.

A FINAL WORD ON INTERORGANIZATIONAL RELATIONS

This chapter has highlighted the interorganizational elements that must be given priority by the agency administrator. The environment in this discussion is not viewed as context but as organically linked to the internal operations of the agency. It requires proactive leadership. Because an enormous amount of expertise is required, it is essential that the administrator maintain an open and flexible posture, recognizing that the use of experts is appropriate and desirable.

9
Obtaining Financial Resources

Garnering financial resources is a central concern of all institutions in American society and a primary responsibility of the social work administrator. Understanding this function is vital for administrative decision making and for the survival of a social service agency. This chapter discusses some of the critical issues related to financial resources from both historical and policy points of view.

THE HISTORICAL CONTEXT

From the inception of the voluntary sector, resource mobilization has commanded attention among social service agencies as they struggled for fiscal survival. In earlier years, the individual agencies had little hope of attracting support from beyond their own constituencies. Wealthy board members and their contacts were the primary sources of funds. This leadership of the board in raising funds is characteristic of the self-interest stage, stage 1 of agency development.

The advent of community-based United Way agencies consolidated fund-raising activities in the voluntary sector. Several fundamental changes occurred. First, donors were separated from the services that their money supported, creating a less personal relationship between the donor and the donee. Second, planning shifted from the individual agencies, which had managed their own fund-raising efforts and internal agency allocations, to the United Way agencies, which had communitywide orientations and had to develop mechanisms for broad fund-raising efforts and criteria for distributing funds among all the member agencies. Thus, while retaining responsibility for their agencies' fiscal solvency, the boards of directors of individual agencies became removed from fund-raising activities.

All this activity was in the voluntary sector, however; public and private funds were clearly separate, with little intermixing until the antipoverty legislation of the 1960s. At that time a radical transformation took place; the federal government made a complete about-face from its clearly defined position of noninvolvement with the voluntary sector. An extensive pattern of public funding developed in the forms of grants, contracts, and purchase of services, which nurtured and supported the voluntary sector for almost 2 decades.

Not only was the voluntary sector changed as a result of this new posture, but the public sector was changed as well. New needs were identified, new structures were developed, new populations were served, and new expectations emerged.

Whereas the boards of directors had previously been in charge of obtaining financial resources, the administrators became central figures in this function for the first time. This is consistent with stage 2 of the model of social agency development, professionalism, in which the administrator becomes the key actor in decision making in most policy areas, including decision making on how to obtain funding. This is not surprising because the skills necessary to obtain funds became based on professional expertise, in contrast to the earlier use of personal contacts.

It took many years for this enlargement of the administrator's function to be recognized clearly. What neither the administrators nor the boards of directors realized was that it was no longer merely a question of obtaining funds or seeing that the books were balanced. They overlooked the importance of understanding the relationship between the public policy intent and the voluntary agency purpose. It became essential to examine the consequences of public policy and its program implications, and all too often this leadership function did not take place. It became a hit-or-miss relationship based on financial exigencies.

PUBLIC FUNDS AND PRIVATE AGENCIES

Because there was little experience up to the late 1960s to guide administrators or agency boards in the use of public funds, the challenge was to establish new relationships between the voluntary and public social service agencies (Lourie, 1970). Several issues began to appear in the professional literature at that time concerning public-

This discussion on public funds and private agencies is based on an article by Perlmutter (1971). Appropriately, when it was published, the journal in which the article appeared identified it in the Contents as "of special interest to boards."

private relationships, regardless of field of service, type of fiscal arrangement (Selig et al., 1963), or national organizational commitment (Family Service of America, 1960). These same issues are still important in illustrating the questions administrators must grapple with in the decision-making process:

• Can the private agency retain its autonomy if it accepts public funds? Specifically, will agency policy be determined by the government because of its financial and other stipulations? Is there a relationship between the amount of money accepted and agency policy?

• What is the effect of public funds on the involvement in and responsibility for social welfare by the private sector? Specifically, will the participation of lay citizens on boards be retained? Will the voluntary federated financing bodies (for example, United Way) continue their financial commitment?

•What is the effect of public support on the quality of professional services? Specifically, will private services be enriched by extending mass services? Will public programs suffer because of a lessened interest in that sector by lay and professional leadership?

Results of a national study (Perlmutter, 1971) suggested the following analysis. First, public funds for welfare services are necessary to meet social needs; the voluntary sector is not able either to support its existing programs or to make necessary expansions in its services. It is no longer a question of whether public funds should be accepted but how they should be accepted.

Second, the issue is not public versus private responsibility for social welfare, but public and private responsibility for social welfare. Both the voluntary and governmental agencies benefit from the exchange. Although there may be problems and tensions, in the long run the social gains will offset the losses, provided that the public commitment is serious.

Third, voluntary agencies can retain their autonomy if they are clear about their objectives and their system's requirements. Otherwise, the available public funds could serve to stimulate unplanned and irrational agency growth that would leave social service agencies without an independent basis for stability.

Finally, the lack of long-range and coordinated social welfare goals both at the federal level and among the federal, state, and local levels creates piecemeal, shortsighted policies and programs. To ensure their own stability, voluntary agencies may consequently wish to withdraw from broad social programs that depend on federal social policies and funds.

These findings, which are still relevant 2 decades later, reflect what is grist for the administrator's mill today. The Elizabeth Blackwell Health Center for Women, which was discussed in Chapter 3, again provides some interesting case material appropriate for this discussion. As an alternative agency, its funding base is never secure. Yet, the agency has been clear in not seeking or accepting government funding because it does not want to jeopardize its autonomy in determining its programs. There was only one exception to this rule, when it offered a cancer screening program with a small grant of $2,500 from the U.S. Department of Health, Education, and Welfare in 1976. That was early in the agency's formation, however, and was never repeated.

THE DEMONSTRATION PROJECT AND EXECUTIVE LEADERSHIP

Demonstration projects emerged as a major public policy strategy and a major source of funds (through grants and contracts) for the voluntary sector. Agencies sought them eagerly, often in an indiscriminate manner. Yet, there was little analysis of the limitations of the demonstration project strategy.

Two circumstances support the argument that demonstration projects, in fact, served political rather than professional ends. First, there has been little use of the actual results obtained from the projects, and most of the findings are lost in the files of the various government agencies. Not using the findings from government-sponsored studies and projects, demonstration and otherwise, is a common failing (some would say a notorious one). Consequently, at one time, the federal government was encouraging the development of research utilization as a partial antidote.

Second, the programmatic intent of the active projects has usually shifted to reflect the dominant interests of the political party in power. Thus, the support for community mental health and retardation, poverty programs, and services integration waxed and waned with each changing administration. Current emphases on voluntary and local activities are an example. The effect of this reality is to accentuate the need for political behavior and sensitivity on the part of the administrator. He or she must act in the macropolitical realm with respect to the use of demonstration projects for resource acquisition.

This discussion on the demonstration project and executive leadership is based on a previously published chapter (Vosburgh & Perlmutter, 1984).

Just as important for the administrator is the fact that demonstration projects are also the center of micropolitical activity that involves the emerging organization that is created by the demonstration project itself. This political activity includes working within the larger bureaucratic structure or agency in which it is embedded, as well as with the set of relationships in the community service network in which it finds itself. The administrator must be aware of all these aspects of the job.

Moreover, particular attention must be paid to the rhythm and flow of the project itself. A demonstration project has a life cycle of its own, similar to the theoretical model presented earlier in Chapter 4 of this volume. It is composed of three stages that can be labeled as preprogram, program, and postprogram. Within this framework are a series of tasks, including securing sponsorship, planning, initiation, institutionalization, stabilization, and phaseout. The tasks appropriate to each stage require a shift in the administrator's attention from the macro to the micro level and from the organization and its organizational support system to the community social service network.

Of special interest are the two major challenges faced by the administrator in the postprogram stage of the demonstration project. The first is concerned with stabilization of the changes wrought by the demonstration project, with the object of ensuring continuity of that which has been deemed to be effective. The second is concerned with phaseout, with special attention given to helping project staff handle the demoralization that usually occurs at this stage and helping them plan for their career moves.

With each of these shifts in the stages of the demonstration project, the administrator must deal with a different set of actors who have different stakes in the situation. Because of its tight time schedule and explicit structure, the demonstration project makes heavy demands on the political skills of administrators.

It must be noted that because of their status as exceptions and their access to special sponsorship, extra resources, and, frequently, waivers of policy requirements and regulation, demonstration projects can become a focus of resentment and hostility in the middle-management levels of the larger agency bureaucracy, because the middle managers have usually not been involved in the planning and initiating of the demonstration project. Politics poses special difficulties here, because attacks tend to be indirect and oblique and because middle managers are athwart the project's lines of administrative support. The administrator must recognize the necessity for ongoing communication with the middle managers in the larger agency and build bridges to them at all three stages of the demonstration project.

NEW STRATEGIES FOR FISCAL SOLVENCY: THE LEGACY OF THE 1980S

The shift in the federal government's posture with respect to social welfare had its origins in the Nixon administration (Randall, 1979) as a reduction in the funding and number of federal programs became the clarion call. Full-scale implementation of this new philosophy did not occur, however, until the 1980s, under Ronald Reagan. The voluntary sector, which had been accustomed to 2 decades of program expansion stimulated by federal social policies and programs, faced dramatic cutbacks in that decade (Finch, 1982). Much of the professional literature of the period dealt with cutback management (Weatherly, 1984), because the administrative challenge was to do more with less.

At the same time, attention was paid to new strategies for obtaining fiscal resources. Lohmann (1984) suggested that "the stark realities of Reaganomics have offered unprecedented challenges to executive leaders in social service to develop new resources" (p. 93). In this important and controversial article, Lohmann called for the commercialization of personal-care social service that should be transformed into a "free-standing industry, not an uncontrollable appendage of federal social policy" (p. 101). Only the very poor would receive publicly subsidized support.

Many other strategies were suggested, and some were attempted. For example, there was special recognition of the fact that it was essential for an agency to have diverse sources of funding so that they would not be dependent on a single source, as had become their habit because of the availability of government funds. A recent development has been the increasing engagement of voluntary agencies in profit-making ventures, known as *privatization*. One well-known example is the annual cookie sale by the Girl Scouts of America; other examples range from selling agency services for a fee to developing new services for new clients.

Privatization has stirred concern in various quarters ranging from small-business interest groups to federal and state policy makers. As a result, the voluntary social welfare sector is today the subject of a critical policy debate that focuses on its tax-exempt status.

Kanter and Summers (1987) highlight the differences between profit-making organizations and those in the voluntary sector in their discussion of the problems inherent in performance measurement in nonprofit organizations. "Financial measures are central in for-profit organizations . . . but the test for nonprofits is different: these organizations have defined themselves not around their financial returns but around their mission" (p. 154). Powell and Friedkin (1987) suggest that "as the activities and programs of a nonprofit become more complex and require sophisticated technical, legal, or financial knowledge in order to execute them . . . a nonprofit is most vulnerable or susceptible to change in both its mission and its method of operation" (p. 191).

The centrality of mission must be the central essential concern for both the administrator and the agency's board of directors. Given the surge of interest in profit-making ventures among voluntary agencies, it becomes essential to critically examine and question this phenomenon, its applications, and its implications.

The thesis here is that venturing activity is not just another resource development strategy designed to broaden the resource base of social service. Venturing activity shifts the decision-making process from a routine management concern with resource development to a critical management decision (Selznick, 1957) with long-range and, possibly, unanticipated consequences that could transform not only the agency but also the voluntary social welfare sector.[1]

Nonprofit organizations that venture into commercial activities usually engage in this new function to support a traditional program that is no longer financially secure by generating revenues in new ways. The developmental model of social agency change provides a useful framework for this analysis, because it highlights the centrality of both the mission of the agency and the role played by the organizational elites, the administrator and the board of directors, in seeking to protect that mission. Furthermore, the model posits a shifting balance of power between the board of directors and the administrator, because each stage of development has different characteristics that require different roles to be played by the organizational elites. This shift to privatization would require the active involvement of both the administrator and the board of directors because, as the model specifies, when there is a shift in the environment that may affect the agency's development, critical decision making by both the administrator and the board of directors is called for at the policy level.

Riverview Rehabilitation Center provides a case study of heuristic value that highlights some of the dilemmas. Riverview's mission had two components: serving the poor and working in the medical arena. In responses to changes in the medical field over the years, the

---

[1]This discussion is based on a previously published article (Perlmutter & Adams, 1990).

institution shifted from its original focus on tuberculosis to alcoholism and, finally, to drug and alcohol addiction. Thus, the treatment orientation has always remained central, consistently serving the poor.

In the 1980s, the dilemma arose when it was clear that Riverview could not survive if it continued to serve only the medically indigent who were supported by medical assistance. Because Riverview was forced to find new fiscal mechanisms for survival, the board of directors responded by broadening the definition of client eligibility to include the nonpoor. The board was clearly committed to protecting the original population, but it saw the expansion as a necessity. By allocating about 30 percent of its beds to paying clients, it was able to accomplish this objective.

With this shift, however, it became clear that the hospital had begun to shed its image as an institution for the indigent. Indeed, a new element entered into the equation as Riverview moved into commercial activity. In contrast to the model that suggests that the administrator must be ready to share power with the board of directors in a time of change, in this case, the diminution of professional control did not necessarily lead to increasing board power. In fact, the locus of authority to define the clients' needs and to shape the services of the agency appeared to shift outside the agency.

Preliminary research on the consequences of profit-making ventures on nonprofit voluntary agencies suggests that an unanticipated consequence of the privatization process can be a shift or a dramatic alteration of the traditional evolutionary model of agency growth and development. What may emerge is that it will not be the customer-client, the administrator, or the board of directors who determines the nature of the professional service. The decision-making process is at risk of being removed from the hands of the traditional central social service agency actors and being placed in the hands of the third-party payers, whose stake is fiscal efficiency rather than service effectiveness.

Previous research suggests that an agency's dependence on external sources of funding does not necessarily undermine its capacity to direct itself and pursue its own mission. The grant economy in which nonprofit organizations have operated for the past 30 years leaves considerable room for asserting the agency's priorities (Perlmutter, 1971). It appears, however, that dependence on commercial ventures to generate revenues may entail a greater loss of organizational autonomy than does dependence on government grants, which are selected and shaped by the agency.

It thus becomes clear that the administrator and the board of directors must remain ever diligent in ensuring that the mix that protects both its target population and the agency's mission remains. If this oversight function were to be abandoned, the system would indeed be transformed.

This is clearly an area for further study, because there is little empirical research on the impact of for-profit ventures or third-party payers on voluntary social agencies. Unless the risks are understood and appropriate decisions that are based on knowledge and experience are made, a transformation of the voluntary sector may indeed take place. Within the framework of social work values, this would be a great loss.

A FINAL WORD ON OBTAINING FINANCIAL RESOURCES

This overview of the changing history of obtaining financial resources is intended to help the reader understand the centrality of this activity in the work of the agency administrator. It is a challenging and stimulating area that is full of *sturm und drang* (storm and stress), but it is also an opportunity for creative leadership, provided it is based on careful analysis, skillful planning, and the involvement of appropriate actors in the agency's internal and external system.

10

The Dilemmas of Middle Management

The route to administration usually begins with a promotion from front-line practice to middle management. Although the major thrust of this volume is to acquaint the reader with the functions of central administration, this chapter addresses the middle manager.

It has been noted that the major organizing principle for central administration is an external one, because administrators are affected by an array of requirements and pressures from sources in the environment such as changing public policy, grant and contract requirements, and state and local politics. In Katz and Kahn's (1966) terms, the focus is on the "boundary systems."

In contrast to the external orientation in the discussion of the administrator, the major organizing principle of a discussion of middle management is an internal one: the middle manager is the linch pin within the system, works totally on the inside, and consequently has no place to hide or escape. The organizational change function of middle managers is consequently circumscribed and complex, creating a middle management bind.

There are three major types of constraints experienced by middle management within the agency system. Each of these constraints is discussed, and the discussion is illustrated and clarified through the use of case material. Specific strategies are suggested that will aid middle managers not only in exhibiting effective individual performance, but also in creating a more effective organizational structure.

THE ENVIRONMENTAL CONTEXT

Before discussing middle management, it is necessary to examine the context within which the middle management bind exists.

This chapter is based on a previously published paper (Perlmutter, 1983).

Administrative Practice Perspectives

This bind embodies the culmination of 2 decades of radical shifts in the nation's attitudes and policies in social welfare.

Until the 1960s social work was practiced primarily in private agencies; the environment was a stable one, and a feeling of pride, satisfaction, and expansion infused the profession. During that period, the promotion to supervisor or middle manager was the reward for being a good practitioner. If anyone experienced a bind, it was the front-line worker, who was caught between client and supervisor demands.

By the 1960s all this had changed. Although change is inevitable in any system, the problem that confronted social work during that period was that the change was never in any consistent direction; it was more like an uncontrolled ping-pong game than a climb up Mount Everest.

In the 1960s there was a major shift in social work practice to the public sector; the practice of social work in small protected settings in which similar values informed all parts of the agency system was a thing of the past. The civil rights movement and the antipoverty program raised challenging questions regarding the profession. First, identification of the social worker with the social service agency function was viewed as incompatible with the primary requirement of meeting client needs. Second, the constraints of professionalism were questioned, as exemplified by French (1967), who viewed social work as "closer to the social-movement end of the continuum than to the 'professional' end" (p. 18). Third, new recruits into social work were frequently products of the counterculture who were ready to reject traditional forms of practice in their quest for a more equitable society (Roszak, 1969). Finally, the new publicly funded programs stimulated a new debate concerning the form and function of supervision in a radically revised context.

Professionals in middle management positions were directly affected by these external challenges that required internal responses. First, client needs as opposed to agency requirements were pushed into an ascendant position (Marris & Rein, 1967; Piven & Cloward, 1977). Second, the social concerns of clients replaced the concentration on psychological problems (Middleman & Goldberg, 1974). Third, middle managers had to explore new practice approaches. Fourth, supervisees no longer passively accepted their supervisors' precepts as they questioned both the form and content of supervision.

The overriding, unifying theme and thrust of all these elements was for service effectiveness. Social work responded to this challenge by a critical self-examination. One major corrective mechanism was placed within the context of the bureaucracies in which social work was practiced. Weissman (1973) sought methods to counter agency mismanagement, whereas Brager and Holloway (1978) and Patti and Resnick (1980) sought to stimulate social workers to mobilize themselves to change the organization from within.

In the 1970s a different spirit prevailed as social work was confronted by the age of accountability. Calls for service effectiveness gave way to calls for service efficiency (Newman & Turem, 1974). Middle managers were confronted with a host of new demands, new requirements, new pressures, and new resistances as the actual nitty-gritty of accountability implementation was thrust at them, which was a far cry indeed from the pressures of the 1960s.

While attempting to grapple with both effectiveness and efficiency in their jobs, middle managers were swept away by yet another shift—analogous more to a tidal wave than to a ping-pong game or a mountain climb. This shift was the wave of the 1980s with its mammoth cuts, reductions in force, and phaseouts, which middle managers had to implement and deal with either at the front line or very close to it. Holloway's (1980) apt description of middle managers as being caught "between two cultures—the culture of bureaucracy and the culture of service provision" (p. 6) must have been seen as an even more difficult problem, given the neoconservative environment.

It is not surprising that despair, depression, and self-denigration ran rampant in this cohort. The challenge remained to enable this important professional group to be effective in its performance as professionals who functioned within human service agencies while at the same time to meet personal needs for positive self-evaluation.

CONSTRAINTS ON MIDDLE MANAGEMENT

A discussion of constraints on middle management facilitates an understanding of the pressures and problems experienced by these professionals and can serve as a critical first step in developing a strategy for effective performance (Broskowski & Baker, 1974). Three types of constraints on middle management—professional, organizational, and personal—are discussed here. Although there is overlap between and among these three constraints, for heuristic purposes each constraint is identified and discussed and then illustrated with case material from a public, county-based child welfare agency that offers services to dependent, neglected, or court-referred children and youths.

Professional Constraints

The issue of professionalism in social work and the human services has been discussed in the literature (Goode, 1969; Rose, 1974).

This discussion focuses on three variables that are often associated with professionals in social work: values, skill, and knowledge (Council on Social Work Education, 1982). Shapira (1971) explores their relevance to administration:

> The more the post-industrial society depends upon knowledge and technology, the sooner the welfare system will be confronted with the necessity of creating structures that generate knowledge, produce competence, and institutionalize channels whereby this knowledge and competence can be translated into means for accomplishing social goals and for meeting the needs of individuals effectively. . . . Commitment to values will have to be supplemented by development of technologies which can control the processes by which the system implements the values, measures its performance, and emulates its results. This implies a changing relationship between ideology and competence as a dynamic ingredient of social change and social reform. (p. 59)

Middle managers in social service agencies are placed in a bind as their social work values run counter to those of the community. For example, the child welfare agency described as follows was placed at great risk ideologically as the broader community, which gave it both sanction and support, withdrew its commitment to the welfare of children in exchange for a commitment to a Proposition 13–type tax economy, which placed a cap on property taxes. Although ostensibly the strategy for providing services to children in their own homes, as opposed to placement, was trumpeted as the preferred route for the sake of the children, thereby supporting professional values, when push came to shove, funding was the dominant force even when it was clearly detrimental to the children. Although the executive director of the agency was active in dealing with the external boundary system, it was the middle manager who had to operationalize this incompatible ideology within the agency (that is, of saving money) and confront front-line staff and clients directly.

The skill requirement within this discussion of professional constraints created a bind because this cohort of workers was not prepared technically to do the work. The middle managers in this setting were in a bind because the job expectations continuously expanded as the funding decreased. Although the agency closed one of its three branch offices as well its emergency shelter, the needs in the community did not shrink proportionately; consequently, the remaining two branch offices picked up the extra load. The middle managers were running themselves ragged as they continued to function as they had in the previous context, because they did not have the appropriate administrative tools at their disposal to conceptualize a different design for their work. Thus, for example, they continued to do individual supervision because this was the way it had always been done and this was the way they had been trained—except that now there were simply not enough hours in the day, or days in the week, to meet the numerous new demands made upon them.

The final variable within the discussion of professionalism relates to knowledge, in this case, an understanding of the constantly changing public policies that guide the practice of the public social service agencies. Given the turbulence of the current human service environment, administrators face the dual dilemma of processing and refining an enormous amount of information from the environment as well as developing appropriate mechanisms for the transmission of this information to the relevant staff members.

This discussion of professional constraints, as illustrated by the problems in values, skill, and knowledge, serves to emphasize Shapira's (1971) point that there must be "a changing relationship between ideology and competence as a dynamic ingredient of social change and social reform" (p. 59). The implications of this discussion for strategies for change are discussed below.

Organizational Constraints

An understanding of organizational constraints from a theoretical perspective should provide middle managers with a way of dealing with the structure and the dynamics of their social service systems. Four types of organizational constraints are presented here: (1) the nature of the agency's purpose, (2) the organization as an unstable system, (3) the expectations of superordinates (that is, central administration), and (4) the expectations of subordinates.

The first, and major, organizational constraint is that of agency purpose, in that social agencies must deal with the most complex, intractable social problems in society, and the organization, by its very nature, bears a special burden. In most public agencies, the middle managers are always on call lest an emergency arise, and emergencies are certainly far from being the exception.

The second organizational constraint is that of an unstable system, meaning that it is impossible to work with the assurance and support of a steady, ongoing working structure. Carefully and systematically developed plans, procedures, and practices can be obsolete within an exceedingly short time. The problem was identified previously as it affected the middle managers' technical competence; here the focus is on the organizational dilemmas created by the frequent cuts and reorganizations, such as staff cuts and the resulting restructuring of jobs.

The third organizational constraint results from the expectations placed on middle managers by central administration. The pressures experienced by central administration often cause it to impose unrealistic expectations and demands on middle management in response to its own administrative bind. Too often, there is a weak relationship between the two groups, leading to little communication as well as a great deal of frustration and hostility. Each group views the other as insensitive, unresponsive, and even incompetent. There is little opportunity for each group to view the situation from the other's perspective. Consequently, the bind becomes more constricting on both groups.

Finally, there is the organizational constraint created by expectations from subordinates. The existence of tensions between subordinates and their supervisors has been discussed extensively in the management literature (Drucker, 1973; Grusky & Miller, 1970; Mechanic, 1962). These tensions are compounded in social service agencies by the social work values of equality and collegiality, which were further stimulated in the 1960s by the great interest in nonhierarchical structures (White, 1969) as well as the interest in participatory management. Although the effectiveness of participatory management varies with the nature of the problem or group (Gummer, 1979; Mintzberg, 1973; Vandervelde, 1979), the ethos behind it serves to put additional pressure on middle management.

There is no question that organizational constraints exacerbate the bind experienced by middle managers. The manner in which middle managers learn how to deal with this bind is discussed later in this chapter.

Personal Constraints

Although the constraints discussed in this section are frequently addressed within an organizational or professional framework, the intent here is to emphasize the fact that the costs are indeed personal and that there is much personal *sturm und drang* in the process. Although the strategies that follow are organizationally based and organizationally oriented, the discussion is framed around three personal constraints: feelings of inadequacy, racial concerns, and burnout.

The move from front-line practitioner to middle manager creates identity problems for any clinician, whether that clinician is a social worker, educator, or psychiatrist. Levinson and Klerman (1967) present a cogent analysis in their paper entitled "The Clinician-Executive." They highlight the change that must occur not only in one's professional identity but in one's personal identity as well:

> This process constitutes a major developmental transition not unlike those of adolescence, marriage, or retirement. As with other such transitions, it may involve a period of disruption, of depression or defensive hyperactivity, of personal and professional growth. In any case, changes in external aspects of the career are likely to be accompanied by inner changes in personality. (pp. 13–14)

Those very qualities that are supported and encouraged in the development of a clinician are often antithetical to executive performance. The greatest problem area is in the use of power and authority. Whereas the clinician is trained in the avoidance of coercive authority,

> the executive is concerned with the generation and use of power. . . . He may use various means of exercising power, but have it he must. He is seen as more interested in action than in personal feelings; getting the work done has higher priority than keeping the staff happy; he has to guard more against his own softness than against making demands and imposing sanctions. (Levinson & Klerman, 1967, p. 15)

The middle managers in the child welfare agency discussed previously experienced these tensions. They felt extremely uncomfortable both in making demands and in imposing sanctions, and they felt extremely inadequate in their capacity to stimulate the staff members to ensure that high-quality work was being performed.

Racial concerns are ubiquitous in the social work arena. They operate on several levels within the social service agency: first, between the upper level and the middle managers; second, among a mixed peer group of middle managers; third, between middle managers and their subordinates; and fourth, between the clientele who are members of a racial minority and the agency as a bureaucracy. Each of these aspects impinges upon the middle manager.

Vargus (1980) discusses various dilemmas experienced by nonwhite social service administrators, including a wide array of expectations from the minority community, from clients, from the agency, from minority colleagues, from nonminority colleagues, and from affirmative action policies, among others. Chalmers (1974) calls attention to communication difficulties in racial negotiations and identifies the suspicion that often distorts signals and hinders communication.

Burnout, the third personal constraint, is related to the increasing pressures of the job both in terms of the complexity of the problems faced by the clients and the larger workload. The problem is accentuated by poor communication with central administration, as discussed earlier. Central administration was viewed by middle management as being totally externally oriented, inconsistent in expectations, peremptory in demands, not understanding of complex work problems, nonsupportive of staff to the external constituencies, and indifferent to high-quality performance.

The effects of these various stressors on middle management are to create anxiety, depression, and self-deprecation, which are among the symptoms of burnout identified in the literature (Harvey & Raider, 1984; Vash; 1980). Personal constraints are complex and are induced by an array of difficult external realities. Clearly, they extract a toll from the individuals who are at risk in these middle management positions, for they are truly "caught in between."

STRATEGIES FOR CHANGE: THE TASK OF EMPOWERMENT

Empowerment means both to give formal authority to and to enable. The underlying assumption is that although middle managers are not empowered in the formal sense of the term, it is essential that they become empowered, and feel empowered, to work effectively for improvement and change within their organizations. This focus on empowerment is based on Maslow's (1976) assumption that humans like to participate in their own fate, that given sufficient information they will make wise decisions about their own lives—that they prefer to have a say in everything that affects their future.

Thus, an empowered middle manager would be particularly sensitive to the continuous internal and external shifts affecting clients, services, and the agency. The empowered middle manager would assume an initiating role in relation to these various events to fine-tune the services on a continuing basis to meet client needs. The empowered middle manager would provide an environment that would stimulate professionals at all levels in the organization to take more responsibility for their own performance, growth, and development. Finally, the empowered middle manager would use his or her position to advocate with central administration for necessary change.

Empowerment is based on three assumptions. First, it is essential to understand the situation at a conceptual level as a first step to deal with it. Second, although conceptual clarity is necessary, it is insufficient and must be accompanied by technical clarity (that is, the nitty-gritty of how to do it). Third, the strategies to be developed must be appropriate and compatible with the individual's position in the organization.

This discussion of strategies is organized and derived from the professional, organizational, and personal constraints identified previously. The strategies are designed to deal with three levels within the organization. Middle managers must learn how to work effectively with their own peer group (that is, other middle managers). Middle managers must learn how to take the initiative in defining their needs with central administration. Finally, middle managers must learn how to work effectively with line staff (that is, their supervisees). It is important to realize that these strategies can only be successful if they are developed within a context of overall organizational empowerment involving all levels of the organization (that is, top management, middle management, line workers, and clients).

Professional Strategies

Values, skills, and knowledge were identified earlier as professional constraints on middle management. In regard to values, the ideological tensions experienced by middle managers are never unique only to them but affect workers at all levels of the agency. Middle management is certainly in the position to initiate and organize educational programs (for example, values clarification sessions) for themselves, their supervisees, and central administration. Thus, they can have an impact on the total agency system in a critical way as they identify and clarify the tensions and problems created by the conflict in values.

In the skills area, middle management can request on-the-job training or continuing education to update and improve their technical performance. In a turbulent environment, such as that of social work, it is impossible to keep abreast of technical changes, and it is essential that prior educational deficits be complemented and supplemented. For example, very specific skills in organizing a meeting, setting limits, and redefining expectations for staff performance can make an enormous difference in regard to empowerment and confidence in striving for change.

In addressing knowledge, middle management can request regularly scheduled informational sessions with central administration in which they are kept informed about changes in the external boundary systems.

Organizational Strategies

The four organizational constraints identified previously relate to the agency's purpose, the agency's instability, the expectations of superordinates (that is, central administration), and the expectations of subordinates (that is, supervisees). The strategies that are developed must take these constraints into account.

There is no question that social workers work in organizations that are designed to deal with the most complex and intractable social problems. This is a reality that affects the total agency system. Related to the constraint of the agency's precarious purpose are the constraints created by an unstable system.

A strategy that is appropriate and that empowers middle management is one that, again, addresses all levels of the agency, because the middle manager is in a central position to bring to the surface the problems created not only by the agency's precarious purpose, but also by the shifting scene. It can be helpful for all levels of staff to understand that the problems faced by staff are based on reality and are not caused by personal inadequacy. The simple process of providing education to inform the understanding and insight of staff members of the effects of these constraints can be a meaningful contribution not only to the system's effective functioning but also toward stimulating efforts to make the necessary changes to more effectively meet the agency's goals.

Regarding the expectations of superordinates, the process of empowerment enables middle managers to be more effective in dealing with central administration. If the communications are poor and the perceptions are negative, middle managers should take the initiative and define new and effective methods of working with central administration.

For example, communications can be increased through both formal and informal mechanisms. Middle management can request a regular monthly meeting with central administration with formal agenda items related to policies, procedures, and other administrative business, while simultaneously seeking to improve the relationship by, for example, inviting the administrator to lunch without having a specific agenda. Middle management can initiate a suggestion box mechanism to help central administration be more informed of front-line realities and thus meet a need of central administration. Finally, middle management can request that central administration approve the development of a seminar series with outside speakers from, for example, other agencies or universities who can serve as a source of external stimulation to staff members who have few external contacts.

Regarding the expectations of supervisees, it is again possible to focus on organizational processes to improve this relationship. For example, it can be helpful for all branch offices in the organization to have similar middle management activities. There can be joint group supervision of workers who do the same type of work at all branch offices (for example, adoption or foster care). There can be training for employees throughout the agency, for those at the front line as well as for middle management, to help them to develop their leadership potential and to encourage them to be more initiating of needed activities, such as planning educational meetings for specific areas of learning.

The possibilities are endless and are limited only by the particular staff in the particular setting. It can be a satisfying and stimulating process to empower middle managers to take hold of their positions and enable them to take the initiative and become experimental in their organizational efforts. This approach assumes that not only the middle manager but also the organization must take some risks, because the middle manager cannot do this alone. The hope is that it will stimulate continuous assessment and reassessment in the organization in regard to responsible growth and change as it seeks to provide high-quality service.

Personal Strategies

The personal constraints of feelings of inadequacy, racial concerns, and burnout were discussed previously. The strategies that follow are designed to deal with these constraints and thus loosen the middle management bind. It is important to emphasize that this final set of strategies has been labeled "personal" for discussion purposes only. The label of personal does not mean simply a defect or problem on an individual level. The strategies must be viewed from a systems framework and must be directly related to the aforementioned professional and organizational constraints and strategies.

Levinson and Klerman (1967) identified the shift from clinician to manager as a difficult transition similar to the life development transitions that require inner personality changes. It is essential that peer group structures, which have been suggested for dealing with the other constraints, be viewed as a primary strategy for dealing with these feelings of inadequacy. The peer group of middle managers can serve a self-help, mutual aid function by providing the opportunity for insight, clarification, and education. The support and trust that emerge can provide an important base for this group and can allow more task-oriented strategies to be worked out. When the group of middle managers in the case study recognized that their feelings of inadequacy were common to all members of the group, tremendous pressures were released, allowing them the freedom to explore other issues.

A different approach is required for dealing with racial concerns. An appropriate strategy is similar to that identified earlier in the discussion of precarious values. The entire agency must be the target for this intervention because the different needs and interests must be recognized and made explicit in a selective manner. This requires an array of approaches appropriate to the particular situation. Thus, a particular method may be suitable for the situation in which an African American administrator was fired, whereas a different approach is needed when exploring appropriate shifts in professional service models to meet clients' needs. Even the simple strategy of providing reading material to sensitize staff can be effective, as it was in the case of the African American administrator who was fired, when all of the managers read and discussed Vargus's (1980) chapter "The Minority Administrator."

Burnout must be carefully examined because it affects middle managers in the specific agency setting. Again, all levels in the agency hierarchy of employees must be considered because employees at each level affect and impinge upon those at the other levels. For example, middle managers too often feel that central administration views them as inadequate; consequently, it is essential that central administration provide the necessary supports and "stroking" as a first step. By making explicit their burnout reactions within their peer group, middle managers can begin to develop coping techniques together. Finally, middle managers must be sensitive to and deal with the need of their supervisees. By developing action strategies to deal with this problem, feelings of burnout will be dealt with and reduced.

A FINAL WORD ON THE DILEMMAS OF MIDDLE MANAGEMENT

This chapter has identified a series of constraints faced by middle management and has presented an array of strategies to deal with these constraints within the conceptual framework of empowerment. The issue of empowerment is an appropriate one for social administration because it takes social work values and applies them to the practice of administration.

This discussion is important in a volume that deals with social work administration because recognition of the needs of middle management is a major responsibility of the administrator. It is not possible to deal with middle managers in isolation because they are part of the agency as a social system, as discussed in Chapter 4. It is essential that central administration be involved in the empowerment process to help provide the necessary and appropriate leadership and support.

This falls in the area of human resources management, a topic that will be discussed further in Chapter 11, which addresses the administration of volunteer programs.

11

The Administrator's Work with Volunteers

Volunteers have always played a critical role in the human services. Not only have they worked directly with individuals and groups in human service agencies but they have also been actively involved in policy and governance as members of boards of directors. Furthermore, many who have chosen social work as a profession entered the field through their experience with volunteering. In high school some social workers may have worked in the local hospital, and in college some may have worked in settlement houses or with local tutoring programs.

A critical element in a successful volunteer program is the administrative structure that makes possible the volunteer activity. Although much of the literature in the field of volunteerism focuses on the volunteers themselves, it is essential to highlight the administrator's role in providing a structure that makes the volunteer's role not only a productive one but, equally important, a satisfying one as well.

This chapter opens with a discussion of the role of volunteers; it then presents a case study that illustrates the administration of a program for volunteers; and finally, it discusses the field of volunteer administration and its relation to social work.

WHO VOLUNTEERS?

The most familiar historical association with volunteers in the social work profession is twofold. At the turn of the nineteenth century there were friendly visitors who were active with the Charity Organization Societies and who stimulated the writings of Mary Richmond; her early thinking about professionalism expressed in *Social Diagnosis* (Richmond, 1917) reflects this movement. There were also the early community activists, the young women who moved into the urban areas and who participated in the development of the settlement house movement both in England (for example, Toynbee Hall) and the United States (for example, the Henry Street Settlement) (deSchweinitz, 1943; Wald, 1915).

The active involvement of volunteers as direct service providers in the human services was significantly reduced for 4 decades between the 1920s and the 1960s. This change was attributable to several factors. First, social work as a profession emerged and flowered at the turn of the century, and by the 1920s schools of social work were organized. Agencies accordingly professionalized their operations by hiring trained graduates of these programs (Becker, 1964). Second, the Great Depression of the 1930s stimulated the active development of the public social service sector, which delivered services through the use of its paid staff. Third, the resulting lack of clarity regarding the appropriate use of volunteers further reduced their involvement. It should be noted, however, that this shift did not affect volunteers who served on boards of directors; they have been continuously involved in this role throughout all these decades and to the present.

Although both men and women and African Americans and white Americans have been volunteers, "volunteerism was clearly associated with education, occupation and income . . . such that the higher the class, based on occupation, income and education, the higher the rate of voluntary participation" (Reisch & Wenocur, 1984, pp. 10–11). In recent years, however, important questions have been raised concerning the potential volunteer pool. Davis (1984) suggests that the findings that white Americans serve as volunteers in larger proportion than do African Americans is based on an analysis of the individual as the unit of study. Davis (1984) argues that it is necessary to examine the organizational context of volunteerism and to understand that "organizational variables are significantly related to the frequency of Black volunteer participation. . . . Black populations . . . require organizations that will not only petition for social change but for equity and justice" (p. 161).

The feminist organizations have raised a different set of issues. Given that women are struggling for economic equality both in opportunity and wage equity, should they continue in their traditional role as volunteers? Does this not perpetuate a view of women that continues to position them outside of the economic structure?

These are important sociological and political issues, and the administrator must consider them seriously to recruit potential volunteers effectively. These issues are particularly important as one examines the populations to be served and attempts to match the helpers with those being helped.

WHY VOLUNTEER?

Why volunteer? This is an important question that must be understood by the administrator who wishes to organize and operate volunteer programs effectively. The motivation is complex and includes both altruistic and individualistic factors. Initially, the literature focused on altruism, because service orientations, social change interests, and selflessness were highlighted (Ellis & Noyes, 1976; Schindler-Rainman & Lippett, 1977).

More recently, attention has been paid to the needs of the volunteers themselves, because self-actualization, professional development, and community status have been noted (Phillips, 1984). Thus, for example, it has been documented that membership on the board of directors of charitable organizations provides both opportunity and status for board members who are climbing the corporate ladder (Seeley, 1957; Wilensky & Lebeaux, 1958).

Phillips (1984) discusses this from a theoretical perspective. He suggests that social exchange theory, with its interest in costs and benefits, is effective in explaining the impulse to volunteer.

> In volunteer activities, the relationships between the altruistic (cost) and egoistic (rewards) motivations are modified by: 1) the degree to which the expectations of the volunteer are met (Routh, 1977) and 2) the phase of the volunteer effort (Wolensky, 1980). For example, while the initial motivation to volunteer may be altruistic (to help someone else), that motivation may also be reassessed in terms of the return. Similarly the decision to continue as a volunteer will be evaluated in terms of its costs and rewards. (p. 140)

It is assumed that altruism is the driving force that stimulates the volunteer to become involved in, for example, college tutoring or head start programs; yet, the phenomenon of volunteer dropouts is all too familiar. This behavior is both puzzling and frustrating to the sponsoring agency, and the volunteer is often viewed as lacking in maturity and responsibility.

The volunteer should not necessarily be seen as irresponsible or immature. Often, the attrition results from frustration with the task at hand. For example, the children being helped are often erratic in their attendance, a pattern that the volunteers tend to view as their own failure; the volunteers need to be helped to understand, accept, and even expect this to happen as a reality of the program.

Too often, when the agency has not provided the appropriate supervision or support the volunteers need to understand the populations being helped or their special interests and needs, it is easier for the agency to blame the victim (that is, the volunteer) rather than examine its own role in the problem. Had absenteeism been discussed and interpreted in terms of the helper's realities and not as a failure of the volunteer, and had the volunteers been helped to develop new strategies for outreach, the volunteers would have been both empowered and recognized for their efforts and would probably not have withdrawn from the program.

Furthermore, volunteers tend to get discouraged when there is little feedback about the effectiveness of the activity or the quality of performance on the part of the volunteer. This can be readily corrected by the agency. In terms of the social exchange theory cited previously, without this supervisory support, the costs to the volunteers far exceed the rewards, which, not surprisingly, leads to dropping out.

ORGANIZATIONAL THEORY AND VOLUNTEER PROGRAMS

The protection of the client and the maintenance of professional standards are of great importance in all social service agencies; consequently, in defining the role of the nonprofessional, the conscious differentiation between organizational and professional controls is crucial. *Organizational controls* are those that are defined by and occur within the structure of the agency. *Professional controls* reside with the practitioner and are the product of professional training and experience.

In working with volunteers, and especially teenagers, because professional controls are not highly developed, organizational controls must be carefully defined to the fullest extent possible to offer a framework for effective operation. Through supervision and a clear explanation of the organizational controls, the professional worker must attempt to give the volunteers an understanding of their roles as providers of a service as well as an understanding of the goals of the organizational setting simultaneously.

A carefully defined supervisory structure will offer support, both tangible and intangible, in the more subtle and unstructured areas where professional controls must operate, because some professional controls are always necessary to cope with the flexible decisions that must be made but that the organizational rules cannot predict. That is why some personal feedback and an opportunity for exchange with supervisors, either in individual or group sessions, are essential.

This orientation will enable the volunteer to grow in the role of helper and to develop a more conscious and flexible use of self in relation to the service being offered. Reliance on external, organizational controls alone would prevent the individualized approach that is necessary to handle concrete situations.

To clarify further the appropriate areas in which nonprofessionals can effectively offer service, Richan (1961) discusses the need to combine the variable of worker autonomy and client vulnerability: The more vulnerable the client, the more professional the worker must be. Thus, in a program in which teenagers are used as part of the therapeutic process, the teenager would operate with minimal autonomy, and the children who are the clients would be selected on the basis of low vulnerability. In all cases, when there are fewer operative professional controls, more organizational controls are needed.

A case study of a volunteer program that serves to illustrate the use of both social exchange theory and organizational theory as the basis for the design of a volunteer program is presented below. In relation to exchange theory, this case study addressed the needs of both the volunteers and the recipients of the service. To the extent that the capacity of a program to retain its volunteer cadre and to recruit new volunteers easily can be considered a measure of its success, this volunteer program must be deemed to be most successful. Similarly, in respect to organizational theory, if one criterion is the protection of vulnerable clients through organizational controls, this program was also successful by this measure.

Volunteers to Supplement Casework Service

A joint agency project that was cosponsored by a teenage youth council and school social work department conducted a program that used teenagers to supplement a professional casework service. Superficially, the program was similar to the Big Brother programs that exist in many communities, but in this case, it was the teenager who served as a pal to a youngster. This program, which was known as the Pal Program, was developed to supplement a professional social work service, and the goals and structure were carefully defined by using the fundamentals of social work practice.

This section on volunteers to supplement casework service is based on a previously published article (Perlmutter & Durham, 1965).

The Use of Social Exchange Theory

A basic assumption of the Pal Program was that the teenager would benefit from the program as much as the child client. The opportunity to fulfill an important social role by meeting the needs of a child dependent on the pal would serve to support the teenager's quest for a sense of uniqueness and personal identity. The experience of serving as a pal would be independent of their parents' sphere of influence, would focus on giving rather than receiving, and would offer an object interest outside of self, thus providing important steps in the development of emotional maturity (Saul, 1947).

Furthermore, the Pal Program provided an orientation and introduction to the field of social work for teenagers facing college and professional choices. The active participation in a social work program can fulfill this purpose more effectively than can a more casual encounter through high school career day programs. Because of the nature of the social work profession, unless one is a recipient of service, there is little opportunity for direct experience with professional social work practice.

From the child's perspective, the teenager was closer in age, interest, and experience than the professional and was therefore more likely to participate informally and un–self-consciously in activities related to the child's interests (for example, skating and bicycle riding). Because the child may perceive the teenager as a combination of peer and adult, and thus less identified with the adult world of authority, as represented by the school social worker, a different set of needs could be met.

The Use of Organizational Theory

The program was carefully designed by the directors of both cooperating agencies. Because the program involved teenagers in a therapeutic program, an array of controls was introduced.

In terms of client vulnerability, the least vulnerable children were selected from among those in the first through the fourth grades. Those chosen were either receiving casework service from professional social workers or, if they were not in need of casework service, could benefit from satisfying relationships with interested older individuals. The age of the clients was limited to children between 6 and 10 years of age, and the pals had to be at least 16 years old. This set up an organizational control by having an age differential that would serve as a protection.

A second organizational control was the decision to limit the number of participants to only eight teenagers to allow for close supervision of the volunteers. Teenagers were selected through a formal application procedure that involved, first, their mailing in an application form on which references and standard personal data were given. This was followed up by a personal interview, thus requiring more than an impulsive or casual effort to participate.

A third organizational control was the requirement of attendance at monthly group training sessions and the submission of written reports before each monthly meeting. These reports would describe the weekly encounters and would enable the supervisor to identify specific areas for group discussion.

The fourth organizational control was the group meeting, which served the important purpose of allowing each pal the opportunity to discuss his or her own questions, problems, and reactions to the program. The teenagers derived great satisfaction from detailing their monthly experiences, even if they did not differ at all from those described by the other teenagers. This seemed to relieve their tensions and offered them support in their efforts as a pal. Meaningful material was frequently discussed at this time and served to further strengthen their ability to act sensitively in individual situations calling for unique responses (that is, the professional control area). For instance:

> The child asked if the Pal would be with her forever. The teen-ager interpreted this as mature foresight, and viewed the question from an intellectual framework. This child had just moved into the community, her parents were divorced, and a sibling had died. The supervisor helped the group explore the meaning of loss of relationships to this child, and the teen-ager was then able to see this question as an expression of anxiety and fear, rather than intellectual maturity. The discussion served to help the teen-ager work with the child and prepare her appropriately for the termination of the Pal relationship at the end of the school year. (Perlmutter & Dunham, 1965, p. 45)

Another organizational control was the careful delineation of the relationship between the caseworkers and the pals. Although the teenagers were never directly in contact with the caseworkers and all interagency discussion was handled between the two agency directors, the caseworkers wrote brief monthly reports for their clients' pals, with comments about the program and any relevant material that could be helpful. Of great importance to the pals, these reports served as support and recognition from the caseworkers, thus giving the teenagers a feeling of direct participation with the casework process. In turn, the records written by the pals were shared with the caseworkers and incorporated into the casework folders at the end of the year. The teenagers were not viewed as therapists, and this separation helped to prevent confusion regarding their function.

Other organizational controls served to protect both the teenager and the child. The program was structured on an annual basis; new pal assignments were to be made yearly to prevent the relationships from becoming too emotionally involved. Furthermore, the Pal Program ended in June to coincide with the calendar of the school social work department; and because casework service was terminated for the summer, the Pal Program, as an adjunct to casework, was also discontinued for the summer. While the supervisor worked with the teenagers in their group meetings to help them prepare for this termination, the caseworkers worked simultaneously with the children and their parents.

The case study clearly illustrates the importance of a clearly formulated administrative analysis and implementation of an administrative structure for a volunteer program. It also illustrates the importance of theory in framing administrative action, a point that was emphasized earlier in this volume. Through the use of social exchange theory, the program administrator was able to carefully articulate the needs of both the helper (that is, the teenage pal) and the helpee (that is, the school child), serving to ensure continued participation of the volunteers in the program. Furthermore, the careful design of organizational controls to deal with both expected and unexpected occurrences was tailored to fit the particular elements of the program and served to protect both the client and the volunteer.

Having described a case that illustrates the responsibilities of the administrator of a volunteer program, the next focus is on the field of administration of volunteer programs.

WHAT IS THE FIELD OF VOLUNTEER ADMINISTRATION?

The field of volunteer administration is broad and exists in an array of settings, both public and private. These include hospitals, churches, scouting movements, settlement houses, programs for

---

This discussion on the field of volunteer administration is based on a previously published article (Perlmutter, 1982).

developmentally disabled individuals, mental health settings, child welfare agencies, services to the aging, and correctional programs, among others.

Administrators of volunteer programs are both paid and unpaid, an indicator of the formative stage of this emerging profession. The unpaid status is clearly linked to the historical role of women as unpaid volunteers, as illustrated by the arguments put forth by Braithwaite in 1938. First, she cites the value to the volunteer in that the role provides "valuable training for citizenship." Second, and of particular relevance to the above-mentioned argument raised by the feminist movement, there are many capable female administrators who would not stand a chance at being elected to public office on local government bodies but who have the expertise regarding social service as well as "more time to devote to the work." Third, the capacity for the public sector to hire "administrative personnel qualitatively and quantitatively is limited, and yet, there are many public spirited people [who] have specialized public interests and specialized experience—they would willingly serve as administrators of, for example, hospitals or housing" on a voluntary basis (pp. 57–59).

The backgrounds of these paid and unpaid administrators of volunteer programs are also varied, in terms of both education and experience. Usually, the person comes up through the ranks and operates on an idiosyncratic, ad hoc basis. Although this process provides an opportunity for the creative individual with administrative proclivities to emerge and also provides recognition of these abilities, the person usually operates in isolation and in a vacuum, all too often feeling unsupported in the sponsoring organization.

> Most of the people now employed in many fields to administer volunteer programs work quite alone or with very few associates who understand what conflicting pressures can build up. To survive, volunteer administrators must tread a fine line between administrative pressures to pick up a miscellany of tasks with community relations aspects and community pressures to serve the purposes of individuals or groups. Clarity about values, and great skill, are required to bring all goals into congruence with the idea of service to meet the real needs of persons for whom the services are intended. An organized profession could back up lonely practitioners when pressures mount from either their organizational setting or community. (Naylor, 1976, p. 47)

This lack of uniformity, an identifiable base, or both is further exacerbated by the fact that these administrators have formed an array of professional associations. For example, in the Philadelphia area there are at least three volunteer associations (The Pennsylvania Association for Directors of Volunteer Services, The Delaware Valley Association of Directors of Volunteer Services, and the Southeast Region Association of Volunteer Coordinators). Although these numerous organizations are evidence of the urgent need for professional association and development, the lack of cohesiveness and unity weakens the capacity of these various groups to serve as a strong support for professionalization and status.

These various factors illustrate the vulnerable status of volunteer administration, which is a reality to this day. Given that volunteers are an important human resource in social service, it is important that they be considered in this volume, for it enriches the discussion of the field of social work administration, and it illustrates an important area of initiative for innovative administrators.

WHAT DO ADMINISTRATORS OF VOLUNTEER PROGRAMS DO?

The role of the administrator of a volunteer program is often ill-defined and amorphous. It spans an array of administrative tasks that encompasses both middle management and top management functions.

The administrator of volunteer programs is perceived as being primarily involved in the more widely known tasks of recruitment and placement. These two aspects are only part of what should be considered a total approach to personnel or human resources management, however. Other functions include staff development, in-service training, and supervision, as illustrated in the case of the Pal Program. They are designed to ensure effective and satisfying performance on the part of the volunteer. It should be noted that these functions are associated with middle management, a managerial level that is discussed in detail in Chapter 10.

MacBride (1979) focuses on a different set of competences needed by administrators of volunteer programs. These abilities are closely identified with central administrative, as opposed to middle-management, functions, and include financial management (including fund raising and budgeting), public relations, public education, record-keeping, program development, proposal writing, and program evaluation.

Richards's (1978) discussion of one specific type of volunteer administration, that which typically occurs in church settings, is interesting because it illustrates one of the complexities faced by administrators of volunteer programs. Richards emphasizes the importance of good administrative practice and indicates that it is essential to the effective operation of a church volunteer program. This is interesting, especially because churches are unique in that there is an enormous pool of potential volunteers in the organization that reduces the recruitment function to a minimum. However, management principles from the business world nevertheless are sought here for a different set of problems related to appropriate system functioning and lines of communication:

> Since all staff are as familiar with the potential volunteers as the Coordinator of Volunteers is, they can freely recruit volunteers themselves. In other agencies this volunteer service is somewhat removed from staff and they find it expedient to work through the volunteer office. In a church, where the function of the volunteer coordinator is somewhat foreign, staff tend to bypass the office to fill their own needs. (Richards, 1978, p. 51)

Although many technical areas of performance are shared by social work administrators in a wide array of settings, it is clear that the administrator of volunteer programs faces some unique challenges.

THE NEED FOR A PROFESSIONAL IDENTITY

A professional identity for administrators of volunteer programs is identified as a priority need in the literature in the field (Anderson, 1976; Naylor, 1976). Okin and Weiner (1973) suggest that the single factor that can determine the effectiveness and the impact of volunteers most clearly is the appropriate training of the directors of volunteer programs.

The social work profession can provide an appropriate base for this essential professional development because of the many areas of compatibility between the profession of social work and the field of volunteerism. First, and perhaps foremost, is the dual concern of both fields not only with the delivery of services but also with advocacy (Manser & Cass, 1976). Naylor (1976) emphasizes the advocacy function: "The possibilities for strengthening programs . . . are growing out of experience in community action programs and governmental services as well as more traditional voluntary agencies. Acting as advocates volunteers serve clients directly, help people find appropriate services, or mobilize resources in their behalf" (p. 12).

It is interesting to compare this view with that of Slavin (1980), who writes about the role of the social work administrator.

> Advocacy in social work . . . is normally seen as adversarial to administration, as a corrective action against arbitrary or destructive agency behavior. The target of advocacy action is most generally authority, the "powers," or organizational policy, the very aspects of the social agency with which the administrator is . . . identified. On the one hand this makes it extremely difficult for the administrator to project a client advocacy posture. On the other hand, when deftly managed, the authority position of the administrator can facilitate advocacy behavior by staff members, clients, client organizations, and community consumer bodies. Easy access to board members both individually and collectively places the administrator in a strategic position of influence internally. Relationships with key persons of influence in the community, with organizations positively associated with advocacy goals, and with the media can be used to further client objectives. (p. 17)

A second area of compatibility between volunteerism and social work can be found in the fact that both are practiced in a broad array of settings and fields of service. Third, many social service agencies such as homes for the aged, hospitals, or feminist agencies already have large volunteer programs; this could allow for the development of field work internships in volunteer administration as part of professional social work training. Finally, social administration is practiced at both the middle-management and top-management levels; consequently, the administrative skills necessary for volunteer administration are also part of the expertise that is provided in master of social work programs with specializations in administration.

It must also be noted that the social work administrator is in a unique position to contribute to the effective development and utilization of volunteers. The social work administrator has the added possibility of defining the roles, interpreting the functions, and bridging the gap between the volunteers and the professionals.

A FINAL WORD ON THE ADMINISTRATOR'S WORK WITH VOLUNTEERS

Volunteers provide an important human resource in the provision of social service. Their activities complement the functions of professionals, as illustrated by the Pal Program. It is the administrators of these programs who must serve the critical role of providing a structure to help the volunteers function to the utmost of their capabilities and to structure the roles and relationships between the professionals and the volunteers.

The field of volunteer administration is struggling to establish a professional identity. This is evident from a broad array of activities. Not only are there professional journals being published and professional associations being established but there is also an effort to develop a national certification plan. The opportunities are exciting for the social work administrator who seeks to serve populations in need in meaningful ways, not only in the effective provision of service and advocacy, but also in helping to shape this new administrative identity, that of administrator of volunteer programs.

12

Administering Alternative Social Service Agencies

The decade of the 1980s was a time of proliferation of a variety of new social service agencies that were organized to serve new or existing needs in more flexible and appropriate ways. Although special attention must be paid to the role of all the people involved, including the organizers, board members, staff, and consumers, of particular concern in this volume are the executives who administer these programs. Although generic technical skills necessary for administration are important, this discussion highlights the unique and overarching requisites inherent in alternative social service organizations that require special leadership skills.

Attention to this topic is of critical importance, because the mortality rate of alternative social service agencies is disproportionately high; not only is there a risk that an agency may not survive, but equally important, there is also the risk that the unique attributes of the alternative organization may be lost and that it may become a traditional bureaucracy to survive.

This chapter first presents a definition and description of an alternative social service agency. The second section clarifies this definition through case studies, and the final section discusses the implications of these new agencies for administration.

ATTRIBUTES OF AN ALTERNATIVE SOCIAL SERVICE AGENCY

Most social service agencies in the voluntary, nonpublic sector resemble alternative social service agencies in their early stages of

This chapter is based on a chapter in a previously published volume (Perlmutter, 1988). Throughout this chapter, the terms "programs," "agencies," and "organizations" are used interchangeably.

development, and the social work profession should welcome these alternative programs. The existence of a variety of unsolved social problems served as the stimulus for the creation of voluntary social service agencies when the treatment of these problems and the responses to them appeared to be both pressing and possible. Furthermore, as described in Chapter 4, the founders, with the élan of a social movement, took the situation into their own hands to rectify the inequities in society at large.

Although these similarities exist between the early social service agencies in the voluntary sector and the new alternative agencies, Grossman and Morgenbesser (1980) highlight the fact that the early voluntary agencies have themselves become sufficiently bureaucratized and static that new agencies are now required to meet the new needs. These new agencies differ from the traditional ones in many dimensions; the most important ones were selected for this discussion and are described below.

The new programs are deeply committed to social change; not only are they concerned with changing the larger external system but they are equally concerned with changing internal procedures and structures to ensure a democratic and equalitarian operation (Schwartz, Gottesman, & Perlmutter, 1988). The provision of service is necessary but insufficient.

Directly related to internal change is the focus on internal governance and policy making. Alternative social service organizations are often reluctant to acknowledge the reality and legitimacy of authority and power as being instrumental in the accomplishment of the organization's goals, because the values of equality and collegial participation are overriding.

The alternative programs are designed to meet the needs of special populations of people who are not being served by existing agencies either in the voluntary or public sectors. Usually, these groups possess a characteristic that is unacceptable to or not accepted by the broader society, thus making explicit a set of values that can be viewed as precarious in contrast to the secure values that underpin traditional programs (Clark, 1956). The services themselves are often exploratory, innovative, or both and are unavailable in the existing repertoire of the traditional agencies.

Personnel in these organizations are either deeply committed from an ideological perspective or are themselves closely identified with, or even part of, the group at risk. Personnel consist of a broad range of people, including volunteers, paraprofessionals, and professionals.

The size of these organizations is a critical variable. Smallness is valued because it permits face-to-face interaction among the various participants as well as the more individualized attention given to the needs of its consumers (Kanter & Zurcher, 1973).

Finally, alternative organizations are usually in a marginal position economically because the resources available to the traditional health and welfare agencies, both from public and private funds, are unavailable to them. Thus, Parsons and Hodne (1982) point out that in the design and development of an alternative social service agency, the resource base must be as vital an aspect of the planning as the mission.

These attributes characterize social service alternative programs and are examined in greater detail in the context of the two alternative organizations described below.

UNDERSTANDING ALTERNATIVE ORGANIZATIONS IN THE CONTEXT OF THE CASE STUDY AGENCIES

A direct service agency that provides services to a consumer group and an indirect service agency that raises funds for alternative direct services agencies are examined here. Both agencies were used as case studies in Chapters 3 and 6 and are reintroduced here.

The Elizabeth Blackwell Health Center for Women is a nonprofit, female-controlled facility that was organized in 1974 to provide abortion services for women. It was formed in reaction to the negative experiences of many women in commercially run abortion programs. It is guided by the following principles:

> Health care is a right; the profit motive in health care can negatively affect quality of care.
> The needs of the consumer should be the utmost consideration in organizing health care. Consumers should be active participants in their personal health care and participate in the decision-making activities of the health care system.
> Health care should emphasize maintenance of health and prevention of disease and take into account physical, mental, social and environmental conditions. (Blackwell Health Center for Women, 1975, p. 1)

Blackwell accepts two major assumptions explicated by feminist administration theory (Ferguson, 1984): first, a nonhierarchical, participatory structure is essential; second, the mission of the organization must focus on structural change, not merely the provision of services.

The Bread and Roses Community Fund was founded in 1977 as a public foundation that provides financial support to organizations working for fundamental social change in the greater Philadelphia area. Special priority is given to small, community-based groups that have limited access to traditional funding sources because they are considered to be too small, too new, or too controversial.

The internal organization of Bread and Roses has been carefully designed to reflect its philosophy; it is thus unique in that it practices what it preaches vis-à-vis alternative agencies.

The attributes that were discussed earlier are examined here in the context of these two alternative social service agencies.

Social Change

The commitment to external social change usually serves as the stimulus for the founding of an alternative organization because there is a pressing problem that must be solved and inadequate attention is being paid to it in the society at large. Although this external problem has served as the stimulus for the creation of all social service agencies in the voluntary sector, there is a distinctive difference that must be highlighted in that, in contrast to most social service agencies, alternative agencies are not content merely to address the problem but feel compelled to push for change in the larger society.

Blackwell was started with a mandate to offer women abortion services that would respect the consumer as a person who not only needed to understand the process but who would also be viewed as being entitled to participate in the decision making that was needed in each case. Blackwell's philosophy is explicit concerning entitlement to care, health maintenance, and the prevention of disease. Its nonprofit status was designed to provide care to women of all income levels, ages, racial and ethnic backgrounds, and life-styles, including lesbian as well as heterosexual women. Blackwell works to have an impact on and affect the extensive, sophisticated, and traditional medical care system in Philadelphia. Although it is primarily a service delivery agency, it views its advocacy role as central to its existence; thus, board and staff members are actively involved in the political process at both the state and local levels.

The recent antiabortion activism at the federal and state levels requires Blackwell's greater commitment to this external thrust while it simultaneously struggles to meet the ongoing demands for service.

Bread and Roses is particularly interesting in regard to its external social change function. Not only does it fund organizations committed to social change, as described above, but it is itself an activist group that consistently plays a watchdog role and that supports and encourages advocacy. It is particularly active in publicizing the problems in the community and the activities of the various organizations it supports. Several examples of the activities of its grantee organizations serve to illustrate this thrust.

The Kensington Joint Action Council organized a coalition of 33 organizations in North Philadelphia, a low-income area, to challenge the lending policy of a major Philadelphia bank that did not meet the requirements of federal law under the Community Reinvestment Act of 1977; they won a $50 million, 3-year settlement.

The Disabled in Action, a group composed of people with varying degrees of disability, has successfully brought to public attention the need for public transportation for people in wheelchairs and with other special physical needs.

The Philadelphia Lesbian and Gay Task Force has released a study that documents local discrimination, harassment, and violence experienced by the gay and lesbian community and has recommended various responses, including legislation and police training.

The Action Alliance of Senior Citizens of Greater Philadelphia has played a major role in the struggle to maintain special programs and discounts for senior citizens, including discounts from the Philadelphia Gas Company as well as a special transit program provided by the state.

Thus, the role played by Bread and Roses on the social change dimension is perhaps best understood by examining the organizations it elects to support: All are dealing with complex problems and reflect precarious social values in American society.

Internal Governance

Internal change is addressed through concern with governance and participatory democracy; alternative organizations are suspicious of hierarchy and authoritarian decision making. The system of governance is a critical dimension that requires the most sophisticated arrangement, because it is often the method of dealing with decision making that determines the capacity of the organization to survive. Two dangers exist. On the one hand, the system may be unable to delegate authority to any subgroup and may flounder in the struggle for consensus; on the other hand, the participatory ideals can be sacrificed for the goal of survival. Both Blackwell and Bread and

Roses have developed interesting, complex, and effective strategies for dealing with this central issue.

Blackwell has made a continuous and self-conscious effort to ensure a participatory, nonhierarchical structure that can effectively serve to meet the organization's requirements while simultaneously acknowledging the reality and legitimacy of authority and power as a functional imperative for accomplishing its goals. Its carefully planned system of checks and balances is designed to allow decisions to be made when necessary while ensuring participation when possible.

First, the board of directors has special attributes. It is elected by consumers and is composed of individuals, primarily women, with either special expertise or commitment to Blackwell's goals and who are representative of the women to be served with respect to race, age, experience, and life-style. Furthermore, one-third of the board is composed of elected staff members, and all board committees must include staff representatives (Blackwell Health Center for Women, 1976).

Second, every staff member is encouraged to participate in decision making, and mechanisms are continually being created to help staff members at all levels of the organization to respond to issues that affect the organization. Thus, administrative staff attempt to frame questions so that all staff can focus on an issue, consider options, voice opinions, and arrive at agreement on a particular direction the organization should take. New staff often have to unlearn the attitudes of powerlessness that they bring with them from past experiences in traditional work environments and are reminded of the mechanisms provided for their direct involvement in decision making.

Third, in contrast to personnel procedures in traditional agencies, all staff members, except for the executive director, are hired and fired by a staff committee whose membership is rotated among all staff members on a quarterly basis. This committee also sets the salary level within a range set by the board. Only the executive director is hired by the board of directors, as is the usual procedure with most social service organizations, but it should be noted that staff participation is active because one-third of the board consists of staff.

Although Blackwell addresses the problem of participatory governance in numerous ways, at all levels and on all issues, those cited here serve to illustrate the checks and balances in the organization.

Bread and Roses is equally sophisticated in dealing with its internal governance procedures, which are designed to avoid elitism. Bread and Roses is a membership organization composed of donors, volunteers, and grantee organization representatives. It is unusual in that all members meet annually to elect two boards. The board of directors is responsible for all policy and procedural decisions except for those dealing with funding. The community funding board deals with all aspects of funding, including applications, allocations, grant-making policy, and procedural decisions.

Guidelines have been developed for both boards to ensure representation by people of color, women, and sexual minorities; donors and grantees must also be represented. One staff member also serves on each board, thus ensuring staff participation in policy making.

Because Bread and Roses is a granting agency, similar to United Way, it has unique concerns: a priority is to ensure a broad donor pool so that broad interests can be served. Any person who contributes $50 or more can serve on the board of directors, which is a critical stipulation because more than half of the donors are wealthy. Bread and Roses has thus dealt with the problem of policy and control unduly influenced by a small cadre of wealthy donors.

A sophisticated mechanism has also been developed that recognizes the special needs and conflicts of the wealthy donors who are struggling with their ideological commitments. Bread and Roses has organized an ongoing monthly group meeting to work with this special constituency.

Special Populations

Special populations and their unique needs are served by Blackwell and Bread and Roses. Blackwell was organized because the traditional obstetric and gynecologic services of the medical establishment were not meeting the special needs of women. This includes not only the reproductive needs of young women, but also the special needs of women of all ages at different stages in their lives. It also seeks to serve women at all economic levels who might otherwise be deprived of such services.

Bread and Roses defines its target populations as local advocacy organizations that, as described earlier, are too small, too new, or too controversial to receive traditional funding. Examples of these are organizations that are active in human and civil rights, peace and disarmament, workers' rights, and environmental concerns, among others.

New Services

Services to the special populations served by Blackwell and Bread and Roses are usually not readily available in other settings. At

Blackwell, the original concern with abortion services has been broadened to include a vast array of obstetric and gynecologic services. Two are mentioned here because they are unique, controversial, or both.

The first is an out-of-hospital birth center, which is staffed by certified nurse-midwives, that provides a unique alternative childbearing option. The second is a controversial artificial insemination program for fertile women for whom pregnancy is socially unacceptable, such as unmarried heterosexual women or lesbians. Thus, Blackwell's board of directors has been in the forefront of planning and providing innovations in services that are unavailable elsewhere.

Bread and Roses does not provide services itself; however, it makes possible a broad array of services advocated or provided for by the numerous groups it funds.

Personnel

Personnel are also dealt with in a manner that differs from that used in traditional social service settings. Blackwell provides rather extensive data on its approach to personnel that can be of heuristic value to other settings. The principles of staff participation in governance and the intent that staff be representative of the women to be served by the agency were described earlier. Blackwell pays careful attention to an array of other aspects that affect staff. For example, it seeks to limit the traditional disparities of salary and power among staff, although there are specific and distinct job titles and job descriptions. As the agency has developed, the issue of salary disparity has become increasingly complex. In the early years the differences in salary were minimal and readily manageable; as the organization has matured, several factors have led to the increasing disparity in salaries as follows: (1) the longevity of staff, particularly in the upper ranges; (2) changes in job descriptions; and (3) the addition of staff with advanced training, which was necessitated by the newer programs.

The board of directors and staff of Blackwell gave careful consideration to this issue, and a mechanism for dealing with it was developed in 1982. Until then the only salary increases were across the board when there was money available, or there were no increases when resources were lacking. The new formula was implemented as follows. A staff member would receive a flat increase on the anniversary date of employment, with the amount ($300 to $500) based on the number of years employed at Blackwell. The board would grant an annual cost-of-living increase, which would be a percentage of the individual's salary in odd-numbered years and a percentage of the medial salary in even-numbered years. In this way the disparity issue would be addressed at least in part. This solution has been accepted over the years, and the issue is no longer one of active concern.

Although at the outset there was very little differentiation among staff members and jobs were even rotated, as the agency has grown and developed, it has been necessary to delineate staff roles more precisely. For example, some staff members began to play supervisory roles with students, volunteers, and other staff members. Although this has served to introduce some hierarchical structure into the agency, staff members relate to each other as peers because of the careful and deliberate protection of participatory and collegial mechanisms. Thus, regardless of their level in the agency, all staff members have access to information and decision making and are eligible for membership on the board of directors. Furthermore, the staff committee retains the responsibility for hiring and firing all staff members.

It must be noted that staff participation in decision making is not a process without cost, because it is difficult for staff members to move beyond their particular interests and knowledge of the organization. Often, they do not have a broad or long-range organizational vision of Blackwell. Ongoing discussion and staff development is therefore a necessity, more critically so than for most agencies. The benefit of maintaining the commitment to participatory democracy and governance, however, is the overriding concern.

The issue regarding personnel is less instructive vis-à-vis Bread and Roses because there are only three staff members, an executive director, a fundraiser, and a grants associate, each with a very separate portfolio.

Agency Size

Small agency size is an important characteristic of alternative social service organizations because it permits the implementation of the central principle of participatory democracy. Blackwell has grown dramatically in 11 years. The annual budget has increased almost fourfold, from $220,000 to $800,000; services have doubled from 5,000 to 10,000 visits annually; and most critically, the number of personnel has increased from 8 to 35 full- and part-time staff and from 12 to 40 volunteers and students. In addition, the board of directors has increased from 15 to 21 members. Despite its increasing size and complexity, the agency protects the capacity of participants to have face-to-face interactions.

Blackwell may be at the point of making critical decisions regarding its future growth, change, and development, because it is clear that continued expansion would have serious consequences for its ideological commitments. The carefully designed mechanisms for full staff participation, which depend on face-to-face contact, would be lost, to the detriment of the unusual design of this organization.

Bread and Roses funds alternative agencies that are small in size. The smallness of size of these agencies usually reflects a very specific ideology and a particular social cause that is espoused by a minority and that does not have a large following.

The Resource Base

Resources are limited in all social service agencies, but the situation is more extreme for alternative agencies. Much attention has been paid to their fund-raising strategies, but the problem is a complex one. Sophistication in fund raising and development work is necessary, and care must also be taken to ensure that the mission of the organization is not distorted by the need to raise funds.

Blackwell's funding sources have remained fairly consistent over the years. Approximately 80 percent of its funds are generated from fees for the services it offers, thus providing the agency with a dependable base. The remaining 20 percent is obtained from foundations and private donations. Blackwell's basic strategy is to stay unrestricted by its funding sources to be free to set policy in any direction that meets women's special health needs. On only one occasion, 1 year after it opened, the agency obtained government funds (a minimal grant of $2,500) for a cancer screening program.

Bread and Roses seeks donors from as broad an economic base as possible. Consistent with its philosophy, it values the smallest contributor, and, as discussed previously, it makes eligible for membership on its board anyone who donates more than $50. Although it has attempted to diversify its base of support, at least 70 percent of its funds come from individual donors. Because more than half of its income comes from a small number of wealthy donors, with gifts ranging from $500 to $10,000, it is critical that decision making and governance remain with a broad base of contributors and not just with people of means.

Currently, Bread and Roses has joined with several other funds in Philadelphia that are seeking to be included in the payroll deduction programs of large corporations and businesses. In addition, it is part of the Donor Option Program, which allows contributors to United Way to designate nonmember United Way agencies to which employee contributions can be allocated.

It is essential that Bread and Roses maximize the flexibility of its income strategy to protect the complex grant arrangement it maintains. Although in its early years all grantees received the same amount of funding, the current mechanism allows for three types of grants: (1) donor advised, (2) emergency and discretionary, and (3) general fund distribution. Because donors can express their particular preferences and because there are always emergencies that arise in this vulnerable population of agencies, resource development must be a creative and unorthodox process for this program that serves unorthodox agencies that are out of the mainstream.

It is evident that both Blackwell and Bread and Roses have given much thought and planning to their financial strategies. Both recognize that this is an essential element in the struggle for alternative agencies to stay alive.

IMPLICATIONS FOR ADMINISTRATION

The equalitarian nature of alternative social service organizations, as well as the other characteristics discussed previously, suggests that leadership and administration in these organizations are unique and must be carefully understood and developed.

Chapter 10 discussed three types of constraints experienced by middle management and placed them in the following order: professional, organizational, and personal (Perlmutter, 1983). Although these variables remain relevant for the discussion of administration for alternative programs, a reverse, more appropriate, order is suggested: personal, organizational, and professional. Of importance is the emphasis on personal attributes.

Very special individuals are needed for administrative positions in these organizations, and although the usual leadership traits discussed in the management literature are necessary, they are certainly insufficient.

Personal Characteristics

Personal characteristics were deliberately placed first in this ordering to acknowledge and emphasize the fact that leadership in this system is most unconventional and, to borrow a metaphor from the field of architecture, form follows function. The personal characteristics discussed here include values and ideology, risk-taking and flexibility, comfort with difference, and the capacity to tolerate an economically insecure situation. Charismatic leadership style is also considered.

Of greatest importance is the individual's personal ideology and value framework because the efforts of the agency to create changes in society are central to its existence. The emphasis of alternative social service organizations on social change in the larger system requires a person who shares this commitment on a personal level. It is not enough, however, to be a social activist in the broader sense; it is essential that the particular social problem that the alternative agency is addressing be one with which the administrator is ideologically identified. This is not to say that administrators must be value-free; on the contrary, the discussion is meant to highlight the dual demands of leadership in a cause-oriented context. Administration is complicated enough when one works in a traditional setting, let alone a fringe one.

The second personal characteristic of importance is the interrelated capacity for risk-taking and flexibility. The growth and development of alternative programs is unpredictable and is dependent on a variety of factors. What is clear is that it is not a stable environment. Not only must the leader be able to handle this instability, and perhaps even thrive on the challenge, but he or she must also set the tone that helps all personnel in the organization deal with this reality.

Third, the administrator attracted to an alternative program must be comfortable with difference. This is particularly vital because many different types of people will be involved with the organization as consumers, supporters, or board members. In fact, the capacity of the organization to attract people of difference is distinctly tied to its mission.

Finally, related to the capacity for risk-taking is the necessity and capacity to tolerate periods of economic insecurity. Not only will these leadership positions be low-paid but the total economic base will often be unstable and unpredictable.

Although these specific qualifications undoubtedly limit the pool of potential candidates, it is important that they be recognized at the outset to prevent the personal and organizational traumas that would result from naiveté.

The issue of charismatic leadership is not a clear-cut one, as it may be in other settings. Although the theoretical model of agency development described in Chapter 4 suggests that charismatic leadership is appropriate at different stages in a traditional agency's development, the alternative social service agency is a very different entity. Charismatic leadership may be dysfunctional in this type of organization, because it may serve to dissuade or discourage other participants from remaining actively involved. This is not to suggest that leadership is inappropriate, but only that the nature of the leadership requires careful assessment.

Organizational Characteristics

It is necessary to understand the unique nature of the alternative social service agency to better assess the implications for leadership. Not only is the organization dealing with complex social problems, something that it shares with other human service agencies, but it is an agency whose mandate is unacceptable to the broader system. The implications of this fact of life are that the administrator must, first and foremost, serve an ongoing watchdog and advocacy function because the broader society requires constant education and persuasion. Although in other settings the organization's mission is often forgotten or ignored, in the alternative agency it glows like a beacon to light the way for all its participants.

Related to the advocacy role is the urgent need for constant fund raising and development work. Again, although this is a requisite of leadership in all organizations, it is on the front burner at all times in these settings. The readiness and the capacity to be seeking new audiences constantly cannot be overstated (Brawley, 1983), and the more the search shows creativity and initiative, the better.

Finally, the continuous search for and development of new organizational responses to meet the mission of the alternative social service agency cannot be overemphasized. The agency can never rest on its laurels. Thus, for example, Blackwell's continuous evolution of new programs and services demonstrates its capacity to seek constantly new modalities to meet the evolving needs of its target population.

Professional Characteristics

It is not accidental that the professional qualifications are discussed last in this list of requisites for effective leadership in alternative social service organizations. Although these may be the icing on the cake and desirable for the achievement of some organizational goals and standards, they are not required a priori.

It is important, however, to examine the possible role and contribution to be made by the social work administrator. It can be helpful to look at the trinity of social work values, skills, and knowledge as they relate to this analysis. In regard to values, there is clearly a compatibility in the social change and advocacy orientations. Also of importance are the values of participatory democracy and self-management (Aldridge, Walz, & Macy, 1982), a sine qua non for alternative agencies. This requires that the social work administrator not only accept and be committed to these values but also that he or she be nonauthoritarian and ready to work in a nonhierarchical setting.

A focus on the value of self-management leads directly to a consideration of the knowledge base of social work administration. Attention to policy formation and the governance process is essential and is linked to a focus on working with boards of directors and lay committees. Furthermore, an understanding of social policy and the relevant legislation is necessary, especially because much activity may be taking place in the courts or may be linked to entitlements. Finally, an understanding of the planning process is important.

The interpersonal skills of the social administrator can make an important contribution to leadership in an alternative social service agency. These skills must include the ability to work one-to-one, to work with small groups, as well as to work with broader community-based groups both within and outside of the power structure. Furthermore, mediating skills can serve a vital function, because there will be many situations of conflict that require sophistication vis-à-vis conflict resolution. This is not to suggest that the use of conflict cannot serve a positive function. In fact, this is an area in which social work administrators need to develop more expertise.

This discussion is not meant to be exhaustive but only suggestive of the contributions that can be made by the social work administrator. Other skills, such as staff development, are also vital, as they are in all agency settings.

A FINAL WORD ON ADMINISTRATION OF ALTERNATIVE SOCIAL SERVICE PROGRAMS

Alternative social service programs serve a critical function in the rapidly changing and complex society of the United States. They must be encouraged to develop, but they must also be protected and nurtured. This chapter has attempted to add to the increasing interest in this area by identifying some of the unique properties of alternative social service programs and clarifying the discussion through the use of case material. Leadership in this sector is complex. It is hoped that the analysis presented here concerning the administration of alternative agencies will be of heuristic value as it clarifies the leadership role and stimulates further research.

Part III Epilogue

13

The Total Administrator

Changing Hats is intended to expose the reader to the professional, organizational, and personal dimensions of social work administration. Although these aspects of professional behavior call for new knowledge, skills, and uses of self, they are necessary but insufficient. This concluding chapter addresses what can transform necessary into sufficient social work administration by introducing two essential subjects: the ethics of social work administration and a view of the profession of social work administration through futurist lenses.

THE ETHICS OF SOCIAL WORK ADMINISTRATION

Slavin's (1980) metaphor of the social work administrator as the conductor of an orchestra was discussed earlier in this volume. This metaphor can be extended by suggesting that ethical practice is a sine qua non, as musicality is to the orchestra. Moreover, just as a symphony is greater than the sum of its parts, the ethical practice of administration is greater than the individual elements involved.

Talcott Parsons (1964), in his discussion of the attributes of a profession, identified ethics as a critical component for all professions. Abraham Flexner (1915), in his early analysis of social work as a profession, included its ethics in his examination. The code of ethics of the profession was central in the development of standards for licensing social workers in Pennsylvania. Thus, professional ethics is consistently of serious concern, within the social work profession as well as in all professions, as much today as it was in the early days of social work's inception. It can be stated that one hallmark of a profession is its code of ethics.

This chapter examines the ethical precepts of the social work profession and focuses on those aspects that are unique to the practice of social work administration. This is a matter of great importance for several reasons. First, the administrator is the head of the organization and provides leadership for the total system. As a model for others, the administrator sets the tone for the entire organization. Second, because administrators work in a pressure caldron and a highly politicized environment, they are often faced with ethical dilemmas that require resolution. The code of ethics provides important guidelines.

This discussion is organized around the categories that frame the *Code of Ethics* of the National Association of Social Workers (NASW, 1979). This chapter examines the code as it applies to social workers and highlights the unique implications for social work administration.

SOCIAL WORK ETHICS AND SOCIAL WORK ADMINISTRATION

The preamble to the NASW *Code of Ethics* (1979) is a succinct statement of the purpose of the code and the role it can play:

> This code is intended to serve as a guide to the everyday conduct of members of the social work profession and as a basis for the adjudication of issues in ethics when the conduct of social workers is alleged to deviate from the standards expressed or implied in this code. It represents standards of ethical behavior for social workers in professional relationships with those served, with colleagues, with employers, with other individuals and professions, and with the community and society as a whole. It also embodies standards of ethical behavior governing individual conduct to the extent that such conduct is associated with an individual's status and identity as a social worker.
>
> This code is based on the fundamental values of the social work profession that include the worth, dignity, and uniqueness of all persons as well as their rights and opportunities. It is also based on the nature of social work, which fosters conditions that promote these values. . . .
>
> In itself, this code does not represent a set of rules that will prescribe all the behaviors of social workers in all the complexities of professional life. Rather, it offers general principles to guide conduct, and the judicious appraisal of conduct, in situations that have ethical implications. (p. iii)

The code applies to all social workers, at all levels, and in all fields of practice. It is particularly relevant for the practicing administrator who is constantly faced with difficult choices.

In an important contribution to the literature, Levy (1979) suggests that one distinguishing characteristic of social work administration "is the congruence which should be aspired to between the ethics associated with the service of the organization and the ethics of its internal administration" (p. 280). Thus, the ethical precepts of the profession should be put into practice in the daily operations of its programs. This discussion examines these ethical precepts from an administrative perspective.

Ethical Precepts

The Social Worker's Conduct and Comportment

It is important to emphasize the various elements discussed in this category because they highlight both the rights and the responsibilities of the social worker. Of major importance is the distinction made between the social worker's acts as a private individual and as a professional. In addition to an emphasis on the qualities of honesty, competency, and integrity, it is interesting to highlight the expectations of performance in two particular areas:

(1) The social worker should regard as primary the service obligation of the social work profession.
(2) The social worker engaged in study and research should be guided by the conventions of scholarly inquiry. (NASW, 1979, p. 11)

Social work administrators must heed all these guidelines in their practice, because not only do they have a personal responsibility to function professionally but they also either serve as a model for others or facilitate others' work. If an administrator is serious about the primacy of the service obligation, the priorities will be determined by client need rather than bureaucratic demands.

For example, an administrator in a county area agency on aging was asked by the state department on aging to implement a set of new Title XX regulations that entailed the subjection of all participants to means tests as a mechanism for determining eligibility to attend programs at centers for senior citizens. This social work administrator elected to let the forms sit on his desk until he would be pressed to conform, and continued with business as usual by serving all senior citizens who came to the centers. In fact, the forms were never completed. Instead, this administrator responded to the new requirements by mobilizing the senior citizens to lobby for change at the state capital. The end result was that this requirement was dropped.

In the area of research and scholarship, it is important that the administrator be guided by the profession's code of ethics for a variety of reasons. First, given that the choice of research areas is certainly not value-free, but reflects the priorities and the interests of the researcher and evaluator, the research agenda must be carefully framed. An example of the part played by ideology in the conduct of program evaluation, or social research, is the emphasis on welfare fraud and worker error in departments of welfare as opposed to a focus on the unmet needs of welfare clients. Furthermore, given that there are a series of constraints to consider, such as limited time, limited funds, and limited data, the code of ethics can certainly help set the priorities for the research agenda of the agency. Ultimately, the conduct of research, both its content and quality, is the responsibility of the administrator.

The Social Worker's Ethical Responsibility to Clients

The NASW *Code of Ethics* identifies an array of responsibilities in relation to the client. These include an emphasis on the primacy of the client's interests; not exploiting clients to meet one's personal interests, be it for economic, sexual, or other gain; respecting the rights and prerogatives of clients, especially in relation to civil and legal entitlements; protecting confidentiality and privacy; and providing a fee structure that is fair and facilitates the provision of service.

These all clearly have administrative implications, especially because social work is practiced primarily in organizational settings. Although it is incumbent upon all social workers to behave ethically in this arena, the implementation of many of these provisions is determined organizationally.

The concern with the primacy of client interests was illustrated in the discussion of the position taken by the administrator of the area agency on aging. It must be noted, however, that this illustration represents an almost ideal case, and such an approach is, unfortunately, the exception rather than the rule. The administrator is often caught between a set of constraints in which the clients' needs differ from those that the agency can provide. This can be illustrated by a situation in which state funds for the developmentally disabled were drastically cut and sheltered work programs, which served hundreds of severely impaired clients, were precipitously closed, despite the strong advocacy positions of the program administrators. In this situation one social administrator at the state level began to train parent groups in advocacy and lobbying activity; although he could not save the programs, he could bring pressure to bear on the legislature. Ultimately, the funds were restored.

The constraints on leadership engendered by public policy often place social work administrators in an executive bind as they see the bureaucratic requirements of their organizations conflicting with the professional requirement of client primacy. Although there are no easy answers, the ethical precept of client primacy does serve as a guide to action as in the aforementioned case and as illustrated in Chapter 7 by Weiner's (1984) discussion of the legal actions pursued in methadone programs.

The protection of client rights and prerogatives is certainly an organizational concern. The social worker who acts on behalf of a client who has been adjudged to be legally incompetent, or who is a minor, represents the organization. The ultimate safeguards, policies, and practices in this legal arena must be designed and implemented by the agency and require administrative judgment.

Last, but not least, is the design of a fee structure. It should be noted that the concern with fees originated within an agency context and, consequently, was primarily an administrative concern. Although social service agencies resisted charging client fees for years, the field shifted its position not only out of necessity but also in response to an important study of fees and client response conducted in family service agencies (Prochaska & DiBari, 1985).

Only in recent years has the increase in private social work practice extended the importance of this concern with fees to the solo practitioner. Given the private practitioner's dependence on fees for service, there is always the danger that people in need will be excluded from care. Some practitioners have dealt with the dilemma by referring people who cannot pay for private services to nonprofit agencies or by providing the services themselves pro bono. An additional concern has surfaced recently: that the individual social worker should not receive financial benefits when making referrals to other professionals. This issue is discussed here because nonprofit agencies are increasingly spinning off profit-making ventures. The administrator must be aware of the ethical issues inherent in the process.

The Social Worker's Ethical Responsibility to Colleagues

Although this section of the NASW *Code of Ethics* addresses the social workers' professional comportment with colleagues and focuses on their behavior in relation to respect, courtesy, fairness, and good faith, the administrative implications should be highlighted. Of particular administrative interest is the concern that employees who seek to change agency policies or practices should not be punished for their efforts (Levy, 1979). An additional administrative responsibility is the importance of clearly articulating the structure that provides for supervision and mentoring, employing new staff, and evaluating the performance of one's colleagues in the agency. Protection against the abuse of power must be assured.

The Social Worker's Ethical Responsibility to Employers and Employing Organizations

This section of the NASW *Code of Ethics* emphasizes the individual social worker's responsibility to the agency, with particular attention given to improving the employing agency's policies and procedures and the efficiency and effectiveness of its services. Although this is addressed to all who are employed in social service agencies, it is most directly relevant to the administrator whose primary work is with policies and procedures.

The *Code of Ethics* deals with sanctions imposed by NASW on social service agencies for various violations. The administrator bears the greatest responsibility in these situations and must work to prevent sanctions or to address sanctions once they are imposed. Although these situations are always complicated and conflict-ridden, the ultimate test of the effective administrator is in his or her work with the board of directors to clarify the issue and ameliorate the situation, bearing in mind that the bottom line is the protection of the client.

Similarly, it is the administrator who is closest to the personnel practices and policies and who can serve as a watchdog to ensure that there is no discrimination on the part of the agency in its employment practices, its promotion practices, and its salary arrangements. Administrative ethics are particularly important in labor-management relations, and administrators should strive to negotiate fairly and with sensitivity to meet staff needs and interests.

Finally, it is the administrator who can most clearly ensure that agency resources are used for the purposes for which they are intended. In these times of financial duress, it is urgent that all dealings with funding agencies, budgets, and other fiscal areas be conducted in a responsible and ethical manner.

The Social Worker's Ethical Responsibility to the Social Work Profession

The NASW *Code of Ethics* emphasizes the importance of maintaining the integrity of the profession and its values, ethics, knowledge, and mission. The administrator is particularly responsible not only for observing that the staff members are ethical in their performance but also in preventing the unauthorized and unqualified practice of social work through careful hiring practices. Furthermore, the administrator is in a position to ensure that agency services are accurately represented in all the public relations material prepared for dissemination.

The NASW *Code of Ethics* highlights the importance of ensuring that social service be available to the general public. The administrator can not only be concerned with access to and availability of the services of his or her agency but can also be active in advocating for social policy in the area of the agency's expertise.

In regard to the development of knowledge, the administrator can take steps to keep the staff informed about the latest developments in the field as well as to see that the knowledge and experience gleaned from the agency's practice are disseminated through presentations at conferences and in professional publications.

The Social Worker's Ethical Responsibility to Society

The final section of the NASW *Code of Ethics* is a broad-based one and is concerned with the general well-being of society. It deals with broad areas of concern, including the elimination of discrimination, ensuring access to services, supporting diversity in society, and advocating for social welfare and social justice. The final item states that "the social worker should encourage informed participation by the public in shaping social policies and institutions" (p. 9). Although the focus is on the individual worker, again, it is of special relevance to administrative performance because the administrator is in a position to involve the public. For example, the board of directors is an important channel for public involvement; in addition, the news media are important for the dissemination of important information concerning both the needs of vulnerable populations and the community's capacity to meet those needs.

The administrator must be sensitive to all the facets of the NASW *Code of Ethics:*

> Another reason for the emphasis on the transcendence of ethics in management is that, of all persons in a social agency, the administrator is the one with the least autonomy. The administrator's accountability is pervasive. It is not limited to particular persons or clienteles. Since it is organizationally induced, and since organizations are complex internally and in their relationships to the numerous external systems, administrators are highly exposed to

responsibility, and to attributions of responsibility. Whether or not they delegate responsibility, administrators of organizations are the ones who are ultimately accountable for what is done in and by the organization and its personnel, as well as how and why it is done, and the myriad consequences which follow what is done. (Levy, 1979, p. 284)

A CASE STUDY

The relevance of these six broad areas of ethical concern can be illustrated by a case study. Oceanview is a nonprofit agency that receives its funding from the Department of Public Welfare. The agency provides transitional living arrangements for mentally retarded adults. Oceanview seeks to develop in its clients those skills, behaviors, and attitudes essential to independent living. The service is organized through individualized programming and through attempts to integrate clients into the community.

The staff are critical in providing the agency's services because they create a less restrictive environment with an emphasis on experiences that enhance an individual's ability to succeed. The staff members are not highly educated, however, and the agency depends primarily on on-the-job training. The work is stressful, the wages are low, and the turnover rate is high.

The administration of Oceanview was struggling with the implementation of a drug-testing policy for all of its staff. There were a few cases in which staff used drugs and there also were rumors of drug selling by the staff on Oceanview's premises. It was believed that only a small minority of direct care staff were involved. The administration struggled with the question of whether it was ethical to invade each employee's privacy by testing for drugs across the board when the majority of staff were "clean."

When the rumor spread throughout the agency that drug testing might take place, the staff became outraged. It is believed that no issue in the agency's history ever created so intense a response. The staff felt that their employer should not regulate what they did on their own time. In addition, many employees did not feel it was ethical to test everyone because a few persons may have been using drugs. Some felt drug use was no worse than drinking a beer.

This section is based on a case study by Segal (1989), which was submitted as a requirement for the master of social work seminar on administrative practice.

140

Some of the employees who admitted to smoking marijuana on days off were some of Oceanview's best. Many threatened to quit if the policy was put into effect. This put the administration in a tough position, because the administrator believed that the safety of the clients was the central issue. If staff were working under the influence of drugs, clients were not being given the best care possible and may have been in danger. The administration faced a dilemma: If the agency submitted its staff to drug testing, some may have left at a time when the turnover rate of direct care staff was at an all-time high.

Yet, the majority of the administrative staff believed that the advantages of drug testing outweighed the disadvantages. Their view was that the agency had been lucky to that point but that if drug testing was not instituted, a real disaster was imminent. Client lives cannot be put at risk. Drugs, including marijuana, are illegal, and their use by the staff who work at Oceanview could not be tolerated.

This case touches all elements of the NASW *Code of Ethics:* professional conduct and responsibilities to clients, colleagues, the employing organization, the profession, and society. There were no simple answers. The administrator of Oceanview decided to handle the situation in a participatory manner.

Oceanview has a forum known as "Task Force" in which staff can come and discuss any issues they feel are important. The administration decided to use this as a vehicle both to inform employees and to explore the possible benefits to the agency of a drug-testing policy. Oceanview made clear to its employees that their input was wanted and that drug testing would not be implemented without first trying to come up with alternatives that would produce a drug-free environment.

Task Force provided a mechanism by which to introduce an issue that was very controversial. Because drugs had an impact on the safety and well-being of everyone at the agency, the issue was raised at the first meeting as being not only an administrative concern but also a concern of the direct care staff. The attendance at this meeting was the highest of any that had been held. This enabled the administration to see that staff were very concerned with this highly volatile subject. Staff respected the fact that the administration did not institute a drug-testing policy without first having a forum with the staff. The staff felt that their input really made a difference.

Some staff members actually admitted that after listening to the administrative reasons for developing a drug-testing policy they felt that it was in the best interests of those being served and that drug use should be prohibited. The staff agreed that if an alternative that would reap the same results as drug testing could not be developed, they would give up their rights to privacy to ensure the best possible care for those being served.

It is clear that there was no easy answer to this situation or to other complex ones. The NASW *Code of Ethics*, however, can provide an important guide to the decision-making process. As Lewis (1982) points out, when dealing with ethical dilemmas, not all parties will be satisfied: "Recognizing that managerial choices may detract from, as well as enhance, service effectiveness, every effort should be made to approximate a nonzero sum game resolution of the dilemma. As a minimum, the outcome sought ought to aim for a just and fair resolution" (p. 283).

THE FUTURE OF SOCIAL WORK ADMINISTRATION

This final chapter of *Changing Hats* would not be complete if attention were not called to the world of social work in the future. Because the social work profession is so very responsive to the social environment, social workers cannot remain totally oriented to the present reality but must also be open to changes and must even anticipate changes when possible. Although Chapter 2 addressed the external context, the thrust was on the here and now. In these concluding remarks the focus is on the future. This discussion was stimulated by the work of David Macarov (in press).

A Futurist Perspective

Interest in the future in an institutionalized manner is a relatively recent occurrence. In 1966, the World Future Society was organized, and leading scholars became seriously committed to exploring this phenomenon; other similar organizations are now in existence. Although much of their activity is purely academic, for the profession of social work, the concern with the future is a practical one.

Part of the knowledge base for change that is relevant to social work can readily be identified. It can be anticipated, for example, that changes in demographics will call forth new social arrangements for an aging and aged population. Other changes, however, confound even the recognized experts. Who, for example, anticipated that the new technology of artificial insemination would raise ethical and practical issues by making possible surrogate motherhood? Who anticipated the current restructuring of family arrangements that has become increasingly common when a traditional nuclear family breaks apart? Could anyone have planned for the acquired immune deficiency syndrome epidemic? Who could have anticipated the political or economic changes in Eastern Europe that promise to affect the entire Western world? Although much that has an impact on the social work profession is unknown, and even unknowable, social workers' antennae must be constantly alert to new possibilities.

There are different time frames to be considered in this concern with the future. Macarov (in press) notes that futurists have several concepts of the future. These include the near future, 5 to 20 years; the long-range future, 20 to 50 years; and the far future, more than 50 years. For the purposes of this discussion, a focus on the near and long-range future appears to be appropriate.

This outlook challenges the social work profession in several important ways. First, all professions tend to protect current practice, be it the profession of psychiatry, engineering, or social work. It is not a simple matter to overcome this natural resistance to change because practitioners have been grounded in particular theories and techniques. It can certainly be threatening to require them to retool and reframe. Second, the profession of social work is besieged by the constant pressure of emerging needs and can hardly keep up with the demands of the present. Third, these current changes often require new approaches; the ground already seems to be constantly shifting. Finally, resources are always inadequate to meet social needs, and training and continuing education are often sacrificed to meet what appear to be more urgent priorities. How, then, can social workers be expected to be future-oriented?

Implications for Social Work Administration

Proactive leadership is a concept that has been articulated throughout this volume. A future orientation is most compatible with this view because it enables social workers to be ready to shape their course, rather than react defensively.

Macarov (in press) notes the reticence of the profession in dealing with social change:

> The profession had not always been distinguished in this area. Poverty became a national issue in the sixties largely through the publications of non-social workers, although social workers have been dealing with the poor since the beginnings of the profession. In England, clients' rights to see their records came about through a lawsuit *against* a social welfare agency. Many self-help groups, like the one concerned with Sudden Infant Death Syndrome, came into being without the help or notice of social workers.

Epilogue

Social work administrators are the appropriate group to lead the profession in this venture, because the nature of their work is inextricably linked to a concern with the future. This can be elucidated by several examples.

The selection of the appropriate personnel in an agency will reflect its world view. Does the agency seek to hire clones of its past and present practitioners, or is it seeking to expand its approaches and services? Its strategic planning will be influenced by the variables it takes into account. Does it only consider immediate factors, or does it shape its present with a view toward the future? Its financial processes will reflect its orientations. Does the agency view its endowment money as a special opportunity to make exciting forays into new arenas?

As in all aspects of administration, the judgments made will vary according to the administrator and the situation, and will reflect the responsibilities of the profession, as articulated by the NASW *Code of Ethics.*

A FINAL NOTE ON THE TOTAL ADMINISTRATOR

After several years of experience in the field, practitioners often have the opportunity to move into administration. The incentives are usually great in terms of both salary and status. These incentives, although seductive, are misleading, because they skirt the real issues that should be dealt with in making this shift. The bottom line is whether the nature of the work of the administrator is appealing and challenges the individual to try a new, but related, professional route.

Given the demands on administrators and the complexity of administration in social service, it is essential that the motivation be based on personal interests, preferences, and capabilities. Equal status and recognition should be awarded to the advanced practitioner who is providing the best possible service to consumers of social service, and the decision should be based on an understanding of both the clinical and administrative roles, as well as an understanding of oneself vis-à-vis those roles. This is not a simple choice, especially because most social workers enter the profession to become involved in direct service, be it with individual clients, groups, or communities. "Changing hats" entails some rather fundamental new learning and behavior.

It is assumed that the inclination to make the transition to administration does exist and that those individuals who are thinking about making the transition are seeking both a change and a challenge in professional life. Although there are various ways to achieve professional satisfaction, many of which are appropriate, relevant, and important, the purpose of this volume has been to focus on social work administration as a career.

Four basic assumptions presented in Chapter 1 serve as the underpinnings for the practice of social work administration. First, the route to social work administration is best traveled from the starting point of direct practice experience. Second, the social work administrator must be proactive, with a vision of the future that serves to impel the organization forward to better meet clients' needs. Third, the social work administrator must serve as an advocate for the constituency being served and educate the broader, external community about special client interests and needs. Fourth, the social work administrator must be constantly seeking to empower both the staff members and the clients of the agency.

Finally, the point was made that these four assumptions may, in fact, be critical in distinguishing the field of social work administration from other forms of management. Identification of these unique attributes is a fruitful quest if it serves to sharpen performance. If the reader finds these assumptions to be compatible with the notion of an effective administrator, and if the reader is challenged to try them on for size, it is probably time to take the important first step in determining a career move.

WHERE TO GO FROM HERE

If, after reading this volume, the reader has decided that social work administration is the course to take, there is much that can be done. First, there is a rapidly developing literature in the field that should be explored. This should supplement reading in the management literature. Second, administratively oriented journals provide up-to-date material directly relevant to administrative practice. Although *Administration in Social Work* is specifically devoted to the field of social work administration, there are many journals that can enrich one's understanding.

Third, there are organizations that can help the reader develop an interest and identification with administration, as well as to expand the reader's professional network. This is an important step, because it will put the reader in contact with other professionals who are involved in administrative work.

Fourth, for those with a master of social work (MSW) degree, there is a vast array of certificate programs and continuing education courses. One might even choose to obtain a master of business administration degree. Finally, those with a bachelor's degree and experience should consider an MSW program that specializes in social work administration.

The ultimate intent of this volume is to empower the reader to make appropriate career choices. There is clearly an urgent need in the field for qualified and competent professionals trained in and committed to social work administration. A social worker could move in a new direction while still affirming commitment to the profession. Is it time to be changing hats?

References

Ad Hoc Committee on Advocacy. (1969). The social worker as advocate: Champion of social victims. *Social Work, 14,* 16–22.

Aldridge, M. J., Walz, T., & Macy, H. (1982). *Beyond management: Humanizing the administrative process.* Ames, IA: University of Iowa School of Social Work.

Alexander, L. B. (1987). Unions: Social work. In A. Minahan (Editor-in-Chief), *Encyclopedia of Social Work* (18th ed., pp. 793–800). Silver Spring, MD: National Association of Social Workers.

Alexander, L. B., & Kerson, T. S. (1980). Room at the top: Women in social administration. In F. D. Perlmutter & S. Slavin (Eds.), *Leadership in social administration* (pp. 195–215). Philadelphia: Temple University Press.

Alinsky, S. A. (1946). *Reveille for radicals.* Chicago: University of Chicago Press.

Anderson, R. M. (1976). *A manual for volunteer coordinators.* Los Angeles: Los Angeles Volunteer Action Center.

Aronson, R. L. (1985). Unionism among professional employees in the private sector. *Industrial and Labor Relations Review, 38,* 352–364.

Becker, D. (1964). Exit Lady Bountiful: The volunteer and the professional social worker. *Social Service Review, 38,* 57–72.

Bevilacqua, J. J. (1984). State politics is the name of the game. In F. D. Perlmutter (Ed.), *Human services at risk* (pp. 75–92). Lexington, MA: Lexington Books.

Black United Fund of Pennsylvania. (1986). Public relations brochure.

Blackwell Health Center for Women. (1975). *Statement of principles.* Philadelphia: Author.

Blackwell Health Center for Women. (1976). *Bylaws of the Elizabeth Blackwell Health Center for Women.* Philadelphia: Author.

Bledsoe, R. C., Denny, D. R., Hobbs, C. D., & Long, R. S. (1972). Productivity management in the California services program. *Public Administration Review, 32,* 799–803.

Bowen, M. N. (1978). *Family therapy in clinical practice.* New York: Jason Aronson Press.

Brager, G., & Holloway, S. (1978). *Changing human service organizations: Politics and practice.* New York: Free Press.

References

Braithwaite, C. (1938). *The voluntary citizen*. London: Methuen.

Brawley, E. A. (1983). *Mass media and human services*. Beverly Hills, CA: Sage.

Broskowski, A., & Baker, F. R. (1974). Professional, organizational and social barriers to primary prevention. *American Journal of Orthopsychiatry, 44*, 707–719.

Carroll, N. K. (1978). Beyond parochialism in social welfare administration. *Journal of Education for Social Work, 14*(Spring), 31–37.

Chalmers, W. E. (1974). *Racial negotiations: Potentials and limitations*. Ann Arbor: University of Michigan, Institute of Labor and Industrial Relations.

Clark, B. R. (1956). Organizational adaptation and precarious values: A case study. *American Sociological Review, 21*, 327–336.

Cooper, R. B. (1983, May–June). Market strategies for hospitals in a competitive environment. *Hospital and Health Services Administration*, pp. 9–15.

Council on Social Work Education. (1982, January). *Curriculum statement*. New York: Author.

Davis, K. E. (1984). An alternative theoretical perspective on race and voluntary participation. In F. C. Schwartz (Ed.), *Voluntarism and social work practice* (pp. 147–166). Lanham, MD: University Press of America.

deSchweinitz, K. (1943). *England's road to social security*. Philadelphia: University of Pennsylvania Press.

Drucker, P. F. (1973). *Management: Tasks · responsibilities · practices*. New York: Harper & Row.

Dunham, A. (1941). Administration of social agencies. *Social work yearbook* (pp. 20–22). New York: Russell Sage Foundation.

Elbow, M. (1975). On becoming an agency executive. *Social Casework, 56*, 525–530.

Ellis, S. J., & Noyes, K. H. (1976). *By the people: A history of Americans as volunteers*. Philadelphia: Energize.

Emery, F. E., & Trist, E. L. (1969). The causal texture of organizational environments. In F. E. Emery (Ed.), *Systems thinking* (pp. 241–257). New York: Penguin Books.

Family Service of America. (1960, June). *Considerations involved in the use of public funds by family agencies*. New York: Author.

Ferguson, K. (1984). *The feminist case against bureaucracy*. Philadelphia: Temple University Press.

Finch, W. A., Jr. (1982). Declining public social service resources: A managerial problem. *Administration in Social Work, 6*, 19–28.

Flexner, A. (1915). Is social work a profession? In *Proceedings of the National Conference of Charities and Corrections* (pp. 576–590). Chicago: Hildmann Printing.

French, D. G. (1967). *Objectives of the profession of social work*. Bangkok: United Nations Economic Commission for the Far East.

Friesen, B. J., & Austin, M. J. (1984). The mental health executive in a context of madness. In F. D. Perlmutter (Ed.), *Human services at risk* (pp. 181–196). Lexington, MA: Lexington Books.

Gage, R. W. (1976). Integration of human services delivery systems. *Public Welfare, 34*, 27–33.

References

Goldberg, R., & Maddow, D. (1948). *The limited intake policy of the Employment and Vocational Bureau: A follow-up survey.* Unpublished report, Federation of Jewish Agencies.

Goldman, M. W. (1960). Radio: A medium for the presentation of social work. *Social Work, 5,* 84–90.

Goode, W. J. (1969).The theoretical limits of professionalization. In A. Etzioni (Ed.), *The semi-professions and their organization* (pp. 266–313). New York: Free Press.

Greater New York Fund/United Way. (1981). *Merger: Another path ahead.* New York: Author.

Grossman, B., and Morgenbesser, M. (1980). Alternative social service settings: Opportunities for social work education. *Journal of Humanics, 8,* 59–76.

Gruber, M. L. (1983). The intractable triangle: The welfare state, federalism, and the administrative muddle. *Administration in Social Work, 7,* 163–177.

Gruber, M. L., Caputo, R. K., & Meenaghan, T. (1984). Information management. In F. D. Perlmutter (Ed.), *Human services at risk* (pp. 127–146). Lexington, MA: Lexington Books.

Grusky, O., & Miller, G. A. (1970). *The sociology of organizations.* New York: Free Press.

Gummer, B. (1979). Is the social worker in public welfare an endangered species? *Public Welfare, 57*(Fall), 12–21.

Gummer, B. (1984). The social administrator as politician. In F. D. Perlmutter (Ed.), *Human services at risk* (pp. 23–36). Lexington, MA: Lexington Books.

Gummer, B. (1990). *The politics of social administration.* Englewood Cliffs, NJ: Prentice-Hall.

Gurin, A. (1978). Conceptual and technical issues in the management of human services. In R. C. Sarri & Y. Hasenfeld (Eds.), *The management of human services* (pp. 289–308). Hasenfeld, NY: Columbia University Press.

Gusfield, J. R. (1955). Social structure and moral reform: A study of the Woman's Christian Temperance Union. *American Journal of Sociology, 61,* 221–232.

Harvey, S. H., & Raider, M. C. (1984). Administrative burnout. *Administration in Social Work, 8,* 81–89.

Henning, M., & Jardim, A. (1977). *The managerial woman.* New York: Anchor Press/Doubleday.

Herr, S. S., Arons, S., & Wallace, R. E., Jr. (1983). *Legal rights and mental health care.* Lexington, MA: Lexington Books.

Holloway, S. (1980). Up the hierarchy: From clinician to administrator. *Administration in Social Work, 4,* 4–14.

Jewish Employment and Vocational Service. (1941). *Articles of incorporation.* Author.

Jewish Employment and Vocational Service. (1942, July). *Board minutes.* Author.

Jewish Employment and Vocational Service. (1945, April). *Board minutes.* Author.

References

Jewish Employment and Vocational Service. (1947, June). *Proceedings of JEVS Annual Meeting*. Author.

Jewish Employment and Vocational Service. (1954, November). *Board minutes*. Author.

Jewish Employment and Vocational Service. (1955, March). *Board minutes*. Author.

Jewish Employment and Vocational Service. (1958a, September). *Board minutes*. Author.

Jewish Employment and Vocational Service. (1958b, October). *Board minutes*. Author.

Jewish Employment and Vocational Service. (1960, December). *Board minutes*. Author.

Jewish Employment and Vocational Service. (1962, November). *Board minutes*. Author.

Kahn, E. M. (1984). The voluntary sector can remain alive—and well. In F. D. Perlmutter (Ed.), *Human services at risk* (pp. 57–74). Lexington, MA: Lexington Books.

Kanter, R. M. (1977). *Men and women in the corporation*. New York: Basic Books.

Kanter, R. M., & Summers, D. V. (1987). Doing well while doing good: Dilemmas of performance measurement in nonprofit organizations and the need for a multiple constituency approach. In W. W. Powell (Ed.), *The nonprofit sector: A research handbook* (pp. 154–166). New Haven, CT: Yale University Press.

Kanter, R. M., & Zurcher, L. (1973). Concluding statement: Evaluating alternatives and alternative valuing. *The Journal of Applied Behavioral Science, 9*, 381–397.

Katz, D., & Kahn, R. L. (1966). *The social psychology of organizations*. New York: John Wiley & Sons.

Kramer, R. M. (1969). Ideology, status and power in board-executive relationships. In R. M. Kramer & H. Specht (Eds.), *Readings in community organization practice* (pp. 285–293). Englewood Cliffs, NJ: Prentice-Hall.

Kronick, J. C., Perlmutter, F. D., & Gummer, B. (1973). The APWA model social service system: A preliminary assessment. *Public Welfare, 31*, 47–53.

Lee, P. R. (1937). *Social work as cause and function*. New York: Columbia University Press.

Leiby, J. (1987). History of social welfare. In A. Minahan (Editor-in-Chief), *Encyclopedia of Social Work* (18th ed., pp. 759–788). Silver Spring, MD: National Association of Social Workers.

Levine, S., & White, P. (1961). Exchange as a conceptual framework for the study of interorganizational relationships. *Administrative Science Quarterly, 5*, 583–601.

Levinson, D., & Klerman, G. (1967). The clinician-executive. *Psychiatry, 30*, 3–15.

Levinson, D., & Klerman, G. (1972). The clinician-executive revisited. *Administration in Mental Health*, pp. 64–67.

Levy, C. (1979). The ethics of management. *Administration in Social Work, 3*, 277–288.

References

Lewis, H. (1982). Value, purpose and accountability: The language of organizational intentions. *Administration in Social Work, 6,* 31–42.

Lohmann, R. A. (1984). Resource development as executive leadership. In F. D. Perlmutter (Ed.), *Human services at risk* (pp. 93–109). Lexington, MA: Lexington Books.

Lourie, N. V. (1970). Public-voluntary agency relationships in the '70s. *Child Welfare, 49,* 376–378.

Lynn, L. E., Jr. (1980). *The state and human services.* Cambridge, MA: MIT Press.

Macarov, D. (in press). *The future of social work.* Silver Spring, MD: National Association of Social Workers.

MacBride, M. (1979). *Step by step: Management of the volunteer program in agencies.* Bergen County, NJ: Volunteer Bureau of Bergen County.

Manser, G., & Cass, R. H. (1976). *Volunteerism at the crossroads.* New York: Family Service of America.

Marris, P., & Rein, M. (1967). *Dilemmas of social reform.* New York: Atherton Press.

Maslow, A. H. (1976). Management as a psychological experiment. In W. E. Nord (Ed.), *Concepts and controversy in organizational behavior* (2nd ed.). Monica: Goodyear Publishing.

Mechanic, D. (1962). Sources of power in lower participants in complex organizations. *Administrative Science Quarterly, 7,* 349–364.

Middleman, R. R., & Goldberg, G. (1974). *Social service delivery: A structural approach to social work practice.* New York: Columbia University Press.

Mintzberg, H. (1973). *The nature of managerial work.* New York: Harper & Row.

Minuchin, S. (1974). *Families and family therapy.* Cambridge, MA: Harvard University Press.

Morris, R., & Anderson, R. (1975). Personal care services: An identity for social work. *Social Service Review, 49,* 157–175.

National Association of Social Workers. (1979). *Code of ethics.* Washington, DC: Author.

Naylor, H. H. (1976). *Leadership for volunteering.* New York: Dryden.

Newman, E., & Turem, J. (1974). The crisis of accountability. *Social Work, 19,* 5–16.

Okin, T. B., & Weiner, C. K. (1973). *A workshop for directors of volunteers.* Washington, DC: National Center for Volunteer Action.

Parsons, P., & Hodne, C. (1982, July/August). A collective experiment in women's health. *Science for the People,* pp. 9–13.

Parsons, T. (1961). An outline of the social system. In T. Parsons, E. Shills, K. D. Naegle, & J. R. Pitts (Eds.), *Theories of society* (pp. 38–39). New York: Free Press.

Parsons, T. (1964). The professions and social structure. In *Essays in sociological theory.* New York: Free Press.

Patti, R. (1983). *Social welfare administration.* Englewood Cliffs, NJ: Prentice-Hall.

Patti, R., & Resnick, H. (1980). *Changing from within.* Philadelphia: Temple University Press.

References

Perlmutter, F. (1969). A theoretical model of social agency development. *Social Casework, 50*, 467–473.

Perlmutter, F. D. (1971). Public funds and private agencies. *Child Welfare, 50*, 264–270.

Perlmutter, F. (1973a). Citizen participation and professionalism: A developmental relationship. *Public Welfare, 31*(3), 25–28.

Perlmutter, F. D. (1973b). Prevention and treatment: A strategy for survival. *Community Mental Health Journal, 10*, 276–281.

Perlmutter, F. D. (1974). Citizen participation in Yugoslavia. *Social Work, 19*, 226–232.

Perlmutter, F. (1975). Public welfare clients and community mental health center. *Public Welfare, 32*, 29–32.

Perlmutter, F. (1980). The executive bind: Constraints upon leadership. In F. D. Perlmutter & S. Slavin (Eds.), *Leadership in social administration* (pp. 53–71). Philadelphia: Temple University Press.

Perlmutter, F. D. (1982). The professionalization of volunteer administration. *Journal of Voluntary Action Research, 11*, 97–107.

Perlmutter, F. D. (1983). Caught in between: The middle management bind. *Administration in Social Work, 8*, 147–161.

Perlmutter, F. D. (1984). The professionalization of volunteer administration. *Voluntarism and social work practice: A growing collaboration* (pp. 117–127). Lanham, MD: University Press of America.

Perlmutter, F. D. (1985–86). The politics of social administration. *Administration in Social Work, 9*(4), 1–11.

Perlmutter, F. D. (1988). Administering alternative social programs. In P. Keys & L. Ginsberg (Eds.), *New management in human services* (pp. 167–183). Silver Spring, MD: National Association of Social Workers.

Perlmutter, F. D. (1989). Alternative federated funds: Resourcing for change. In F. D. Perlmutter (Ed.), *Alternative social agencies: Administrative strategies* (pp. 95–108). New York: Haworth.

Perlmutter, F. D., & Adams, C. T. (1990). The voluntary sector and for profit ventures. *Administration in Social Work, 14*(1), 1–14.

Perlmutter, F. D., & Durham, D. (1965). Using teenagers to supplement casework service. *Social Work, 10*, 41–46.

Perlmutter, F. D., Richan, W. C., & Weirich, T. W. (1977). *The political and policy contexts of the United Services Agency.* Mimeographed monograph. Philadelphia: Temple University.

Perlmutter, F. D., & Silverman, H. (1972). The community mental health center: A structural anachronism. *Social Work, 17*, 78–85.

Perlmutter, F. D., & Silverman, H. (1973). Conflict in consultation–education. *Community Mental Health Journal, 9*, 116–122.

Perlmutter, F. D., & Vayda, A. M. (1978). Barriers to prevention programs in community mental health centers. *Administration in Mental Health, 2*, 140–153.

Perlmutter, F. D., Yudin, L., & Heinemann, S. (1974). Awareness of community mental health centers among three gatekeeper groups. *American Journal of Community Psychology, 2*, 23–33.

Phillips, M. C. (1984). Motivation and expectation in successful volunteerism. In F. C. Schwartz (Ed.), *Voluntarism and social work practice* (pp. 139–146). Lanham, MD: University Press of America.

Piven, F. F., & Cloward, R. A. (1977). *Poor people's movements.* New York: Pantheon Books.

Powell, W. W., & Friedkin, R. (1987). Organizational change in nonprofit organizations. In W. W. Powell (Ed.), *The nonprofit sector: A research handbook* (pp. 180–192). New Haven, CT: Yale University Press.

President's Commission on Mental Health. (1978). *Report of the task panel on public attitudes and use of the media for promotion of mental health.* Washington, DC: U.S. Government Printing Office.

Prochaska, J. M., & DiBari, P. M. (1985). Toward a fundamentally fair fee system: A case study. *Administration in Social Work, 9,* 49–58.

Pusic, E. (1974). The administration of welfare. In F. D. Perlmutter (Ed.), *A design for social work practice* (pp. 192–209). New York: Columbia University Press.

Radin, B. (1983). What role will the federal government play? *Public Welfare, 41,* 14–17.

Randall, R. (1979). Presidential power and bureaucratic intransigence: The influence of the Nixon administration on welfare policy. *American Political Science Review, 73,* 795–810.

Reisch, M., and Wenocur, S. (1984). Professionalism and voluntarism in social welfare: Changing roles and functions. In F. C. Schwartz (Ed.), *Voluntarism and social work practice* (pp. 1–21). Lanham, MD: University Press of America.

Richan, W. C. (1961). A theoretical scheme for determining roles of professional and nonprofessional personnel. *Social Work, 6,* 22–28.

Richards, J. (1978). Church volunteer administration: Similarities and differences. *Volunteer Administration, 11,* 49–52.

Richmond, M. E. (1917). *Social diagnosis.* New York: Russell Sage Foundation.

Rose, G. (1974). Issues in professionalism: British social work triumphant. In F. D. Perlmutter (Ed.), *A design for social work practice* (pp. 172–191). New York: Columbia University Press.

Rosenberg, M., & Brody, R. (1974). *Systems serving people: A breakthrough in service delivery.* Cleveland: Case Western Reserve University.

Rosenthal, S., & Young, J. E. (1980). The governance of ten social services. In F. D. Perlmutter & S. Slavin (Eds.), *Leadership in social administration* (pp. 86–102). Philadelphia: Temple University Press.

Ross, M. G. (1967). *Community organization: Theory, principles and practice.* New York: Harper & Row.

Roszak, T. (1969). *The making of a counter culture.* New York: Doubleday.

Rothman, J. (1974). *Planning and organizing for social change: Action principles from social science research.* New York: Columbia University Press.

Routh, T. A. (1977). *The volunteer and community agencies.* Springfield, IL: Charles C Thomas.

Saul, L. (1947). *Emotional maturity.* Philadelphia: J. B. Lippincott.

References

Schindler-Rainman, E., & Lippett, R. (1977). *The volunteer community.* La Jolla, CA: University Associates.

Schwartz, A. Y., Gottesman, E. W., & Perlmutter, F. D. (1988). Blackwell: A case study on feminist administration. In F. D. Perlmutter (Ed.), *Alternative social agencies, administrative strategies* (pp. 5–15). New York: Haworth.

Seeley, J. (1957). *Community chest, a case study in philanthropy.* Toronto: University of Toronto Press.

Segal, A. J. (1989). *Administrative ethics.* Unpublished manuscript, Temple University, School of Social Administration, Philadelphia.

Selig, M. K., et al. (1963). The challenge of public funds to private agencies. *Journal of Jewish Communal Service, 39,* 368–377.

Selvini-Palazzoli, M., Boscolo, L., Cecchin, G., & Prata, G. (1978). *Paradox and counter paradox.* New York: Jason Aronson Press.

Selznick, P. (1957). *Leadership in administration.* Evanston, IL: Row Publishing.

Shapira, M. (1971). Reflections on the preparation of social workers for executive positions. *Journal of Education for Social Work, 7,* 55–68.

Sherman, H. (1966). *It all depends.* University, AL: University of Alabama Press.

Sills, D. (1957). *The volunteers.* New York: Free Press.

Skinner, W., & Sasser, W. E. (1977). Managers with impact: Versatile and inconsistent. *Harvard Business Review, 55*(November–December), 140–148.

Slavin, S. (1980). A theoretical framework for social administration. In F. D. Perlmutter & S. Slavin (Eds.), *Leadership in social administration* (pp. 3–21). Philadelphia: Temple University Press.

Spencer, S. (1959). *The administration method in social work education, project report of the curriculum study* (Vol. 3). New York: Council on Social Work Education.

Steinberg, R. M., & Carter, G. W. (1983). *Case management and the elderly.* Lexington, MA: Lexington Books.

Stern, M. (1984). The politics of American social welfare. In F. D. Perlmutter (Ed.), *Human services at risk* (pp. 3–22). Lexington, MA: Lexington Books.

Trecker, H. B. (1948). *Social work administration: Principles and practices.* New York: Association Press.

Vajs, E. (1973). *Developing social policy in conditions of rapid change.* Yugoslavia report presented to the Sixteenth International Conference on Social Welfare, The Hague, The Netherlands.

Vandervelde, M. (1979). The semantics of participation. *Administration in Social Work, 3,* 65–78.

Vargus, I. D. (1980). The minority administrator. In F. D. Perlmutter & S. Slavin (Eds.), *Leadership in social administration* (pp. 216–229). Philadelphia: Temple University Press.

Vash, C. (1980). *The burnt-out administrator.* New York: Springer.

Vosburgh, W. W., & Perlmutter, F. D. (1984). The demonstration project: Politics amid professionalism. In F. D. Perlmutter (Ed.), *Human services at risk* (pp. 109–125). Lexington, MA: Lexington Books.

Wald, L. (1915). *The house on Henry Street.* New York: Henry Holt.

References

Weatherly, R. (1984). Approaches to cutback management. In F. D. Perlmutter (Ed.), *Human services at risk* (pp. 39–56). Lexington, MA: Lexington Books.

Weil, M. (1988). Creating an alternative culture in a public service setting. In F. D. Perlmutter (Ed.), *Alternative social agencies: Administrative strategies* (pp. 69–82). New York: Haworth.

Weil, M. , Karls, J. M., and Associates. (1985). *Case management in human service practice.* San Francisco: Jossey-Bass.

Weiner, H. (1984). Survival through coalition: The case of additions programs. In F. D. Perlmutter (Ed.), *Human services at risk* (pp. 197–212). Lexington, MA: Lexington Books.

Weissman, J. (1973). *Overcoming mismanagement in the human service professional.* San Francisco: Jossey-Bass.

White, O. (1969). The dialectical organization: An alternative to bureaucracy. *Public Administration Review, 29,* 32–42.

Wilensky, H., & Lebeaux, C. (1958). *Industrial society and social welfare.* New York: Russell Sage Foundation.

Wilson, S. M. (1980). Values and technology: Foundations for practice. In F. D. Perlmutter & S. Slavin (Eds.), *Leadership in social administration* (pp. 106–122). Philadelphia: Temple University Press.

Wirth, L. (1957). Types of minority movements. In R. H. Turner & L. M. Killian (Eds.), *Collective behavior* (pp. 321–326). Englewood Cliffs, NJ: Prentice-Hall.

Wolensky, R. P. (1980). Toward a broader conceptualization of volunteerism in disaster. *Journal of Voluntary Action Research, 8*(July–October), 43–50.

Index

Index

Index

Subordinates, expectations of, 95, 96, 100

Superordinates, expectations of, 95, 96, 100, 101. *See* Central administration

Systems perspective
case study, 27–32
definition of, 25
elements of, 25–26

Technology
decisions regarding, 18
impact of, 13–14

Tertiary (external) constituencies, 26, 29, 30

Theory
function and differences in, 7–9
importance of, 34

Unions, 16

United States
rate of social change in, 10
social environment of 1980s, 65–66
technological change in, 13–14
turbulent environment in, 10–11
value system shifts in, 11–13

United Way, 48, 60, 61, 79, 82–83, 84, 126

Value system
of agency, 34, 37, 39
shifts in, 11–13

Values relevant to administration, 94, 99

Vargus, I. D., 15, 98

Vocational Rehabilitation Act of 1954, 49

Voluntary sector
cutbacks in 1980s, 87
fund-raising activities in, 83
public funds and, 84–85, 87–89
redesign of, 69–70
strategic planning in, 79

Volunteer administration, 111–116

Volunteers
profile of, 104–105
reasons for becoming, 106–108
used to supplement casework service, 108–111

Women
in management positions, 14, 15
as volunteers, 105, 112

About the Author

Felice Davidson Perlmutter, PhD, ACSW, is Professor of Social Administration at Temple University, Philadelphia, Pennsylvania. She received her MSW at the University of Connecticut and her doctorate at the Bryn Mawr College School of Social Work. She has edited five books and published more than 50 articles in books and such journals as *Child Welfare, Social Work, Community Mental Health Journal, Administration in Social Work,* and the *International Journal of Sociology and Social Policy.* She serves on the editorial boards of *Administration in Social Work, Clinical Supervisor, Journal of Family Systems Medicine, Mediation Quarterly,* and *Sociology and Social Welfare.*

In addition to her involvement with social work administration, Dr. Perlmutter has been active in family dispute mediation, in Jewish community organizations, in governmental legislation and policy formulation, and in professional association activities. She has also taught in universities in England, Yugoslavia, and Israel, and she led a tour during the 1980 International Conference of Social Welfare in China.

Dr. Perlmutter is a fellow of the American Orthopsychiatric Association and a member of the National Association of Social Workers, the American Association of University Professors, the Academy of Family Mediators, the Council on Social Work Education, the Society of Professionals in Dispute Resolution, and the National Network for Social Work Managers.